SONGS & HYMNS
for Blended Worship

Editorial Committee:
Dr. Robert Webber, Vicky Tusken,
John Witvliet, Jack Schrader

Singer's Edition - Hardbound
Code No. 1992

Singer's Edition - Paperback
Code No. 1997

Full Accompaniment Edition - Spiral
Code No. 1998

No part of this publication may be reproduced or transmitted in any form or by any means, electronic or mechanical, including photocopy, recording or any information storage and retrieval system without written permission from the publisher.

© 1995 Hope Publishing Company, 380 So. Main Pl., Carol Stream, IL 60188
All rights reserved. International copyright secured. Printed in the USA.

Hope Publishing Company
CAROL STREAM IL 60188

Foreword

In the last forty years of the twentieth century, Christian churches have experienced unprecedented worship renewal.

Since the 1960s there have been two main streams of renewal – the liturgical renewal that draws on ancient and historical sources; and contemporary worship renewal that draws from biblical imagery and contemporary sound.

Since 1990 there has been a third and growing movement of worship renewal known as blended worship. This movement brings together the best from traditional and contemporary worship, and blends them together in a new and powerful way.

This new form of worship is ordered by the biblical and historical fourfold pattern of worship: gathering, hearing God's word, offering thanksgiving (at the table or in prayer and song), and the dismissal.

Renew! Songs and Hymns for Blended Worship has been published to serve and facilitate this new movement of the Spirit and has been organized around the fourfold pattern of worship.

RENEW!

Table of Contents

GATHERING SONGS	Nos. 1 –	89
Songs for Coming to Worship	1 –	21
Songs About God	22 –	32
Songs to God	33 –	44
Processional Hymns	45 –	62
Songs of Praise	63 –	83
Songs of Confession and Lament	84 –	89
THE SERVICE OF THE WORD	Nos. 90 –	194
Songs of Illumination	90 –	97
Biblical Songs	98 –	135
-Psalm Refrains	98 –	102
-Songs from the Psalms	103 –	119
-Old Testament Songs	120 –	126
-New Testament Songs	127 –	135
Alleluia Songs	136 –	139
Invitational Songs	140 –	147
Dedication Songs	148 –	155
Creedal Songs	156 –	166
Prayer Songs	167 –	180
Songs of Confession	181 –	188
Songs of Assurance	189 –	194

THE SERVICE OF THE TABLE	Nos. 195 – 248
Invitation to Communion Songs	195 – 202
Sanctus Songs	203 – 208
Acclamation Songs	209 – 213
Lamb of God Songs	214 – 216
Communion Songs	217 – 237
Post-Communion Songs	238 – 248
PRAISE AND THANKSGIVING	Nos. 249 – 284
Songs for Praising the Father	249 – 265
Songs to Remember the Work of the Son	266 – 279
Songs to Invoke the Presence of the Holy Spirit	280 – 284
THE GOING FORTH	Nos. 285 – 308
Songs of Service	285 – 291
Benedictions	292 – 295
Recessional Hymns	296 – 308

Gathering Songs

Songs for Coming to Worship

O Come, Let Us Adore Him   1

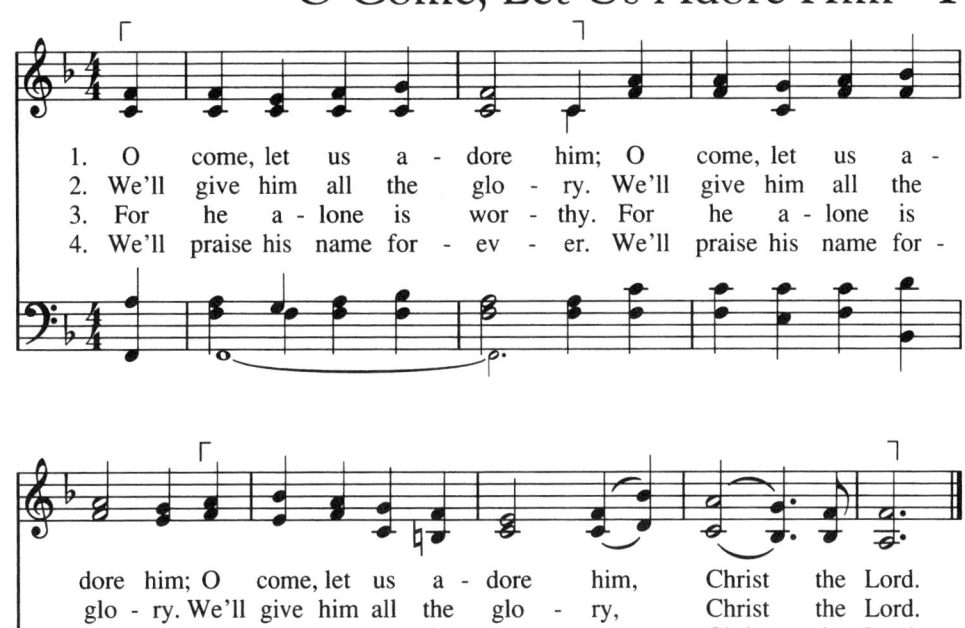

1. O come, let us adore him; O come, let us adore him; O come, let us adore him, Christ the Lord.
2. We'll give him all the glory. We'll give him all the glory. We'll give him all the glory, Christ the Lord.
3. For he alone is worthy. For he alone is worthy. For he alone is worthy, Christ the Lord.
4. We'll praise his name forever. We'll praise his name forever. We'll praise his name forever, Christ the Lord.

WORDS: St. 1 attr. J. F. Wade, 1751; tr F. Oakeley, 1841; sts. 2–4, anonymous
MUSIC: John F. Wade's *Cantus Diversi*, 1751

ADESTE FIDELES
Irregular

Come into His Presence   2

4 Part Round

1. Come into his presence singing, *Alleluia, alleluia, alleluia!
*2. Jesus is Lord.   *3. Worthy the Lamb.   *4. Glory to God.

WORDS and MUSIC: Anonymous

HIS PRESENCE
Irregular

THE GATHERING

3 We Bring the Sacrifice of Praise

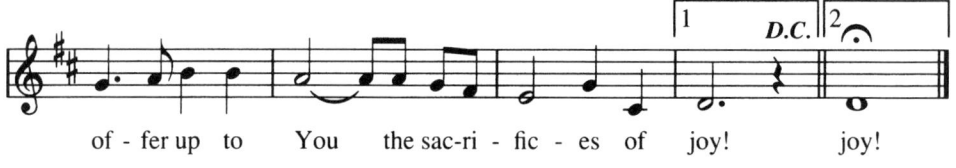

WORDS and MUSIC: Kirk Dearman
© Copyright 1984 John T. Benson Publishing Co./ASCAP (chorus).
All Rights Reserved. Used by Permission of Benson Music Group, Inc.

SONGS FOR COMING TO WORSHIP

Lord, I Lift Your Name on High   4

Lord, I lift Your name on high;   Lord, I love to sing Your

prais - es.   I'm so glad You're in my life;

I'm so glad You came to save us.

You came from heav - en to earth to show the way,

from the earth to the cross, my debt to pay.

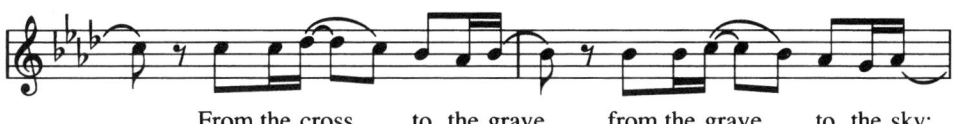
From the cross to the grave, from the grave to the sky;

Lord, I lift Your name on high!

WORDS and MUSIC: Rick Founds
©1989 MARANATHA! MUSIC (Administered by THE COPYRIGHT COMPANY, Nashville, TN)
All Rights Reserved. International Copyright Secured. Used By Permission.

SONGS FOR COMING TO WORSHIP

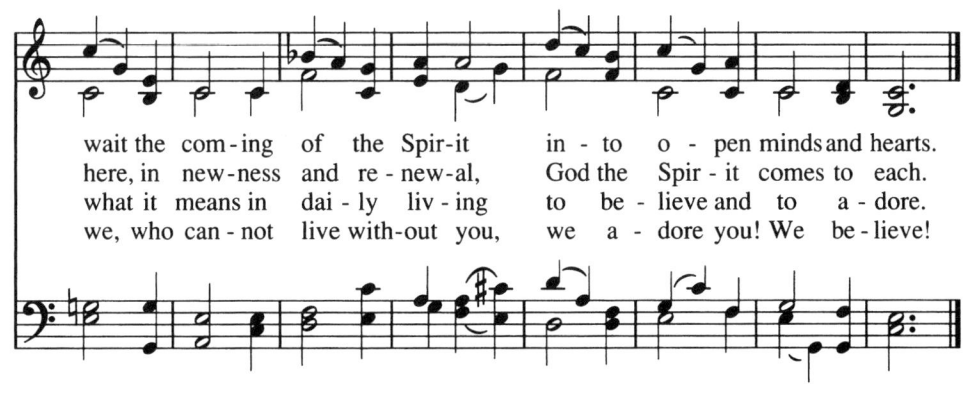

wait the com-ing of the Spir-it in-to o-pen minds and hearts.
here, in new-ness and re-new-al, God the Spir-it comes to each.
what it means in dai-ly liv-ing to be-lieve and to a-dore.
we, who can-not live with-out you, we a-dore you! We be-lieve!

As We Gather 6

1. As we gath-er may Your Spir-it work with-in us,

as we gath-er may we glo-ri-fy Your Name.

Know-ing well that as our hearts be-gin to wor-ship,

we'll be blessed be-cause we came,

we'll be blessed be-cause we came.

WORDS and MUSIC: Mike Fay & Tom Coomes
© 1981 COOMESIETUNES (Administered by MARANATHA! MUSIC c/o THE COPYRIGHT COMPANY,
Nashville, TN)/MARANATHA! MUSIC (Administered by THE COPYRIGHT COMPANY, Nashville, TN)
All Rights Reserved. Used by Permission.

THE GATHERING

7 Praise the Name of Jesus

Praise the name of Jesus, praise the name of Jesus.

He's my Rock, he's my Fortress, he's my Deliverer, in

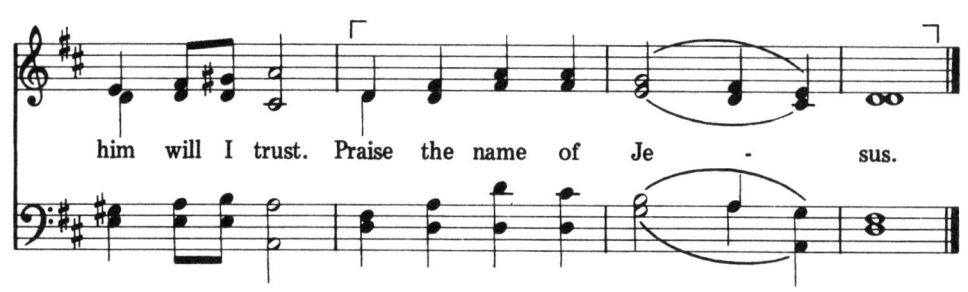

him will I trust. Praise the name of Jesus.

WORDS and MUSIC: Roy Hicks, Jr., 1970; based on Psalm 18:1
© 1976 Latter Rain Music. Admin. by EMI Christian Music Publishing.
All Rights Reserved. Used By Permission.

HICKS
Irregular

SONGS FOR COMING TO WORSHIP

God Himself Is with Us 8

1. God himself is with us: let us now adore him, and with awe appear before him. God is in his temple, all within keep silence, and before him bow with reverence. Him alone do we own as our God and Savior; praise his name forever.

2. God himself is with us; hear the harps resounding! See the crowds the throne surrounding! "Holy, holy, holy," hear the hymn ascending, angels, saints, their voices blending! Bow your ear to us here; hear, O Christ, the praises that your Church now raises.

3. Fount of every blessing, purify my spirit, trusting only in your merit. Like the holy angels who behold your glory, may I ceaselessly adore you, and in all, great and small, seek to do most nearly what you love so dearly.

WORDS: Gerhardt Tersteegen, 1729; tr. composite, alt.
MUSIC: Joachim Neander, 1680

ARNSBERG
6.6.8.6.6.8.8.6.6.6.

THE GATHERING

9 As the Deer Pants for the Water

1. As the deer pants for the wa-ter, so my
2. I want you more than gold or sil-ver, on-ly
3. You're my friend and you are my broth-er, e-ven

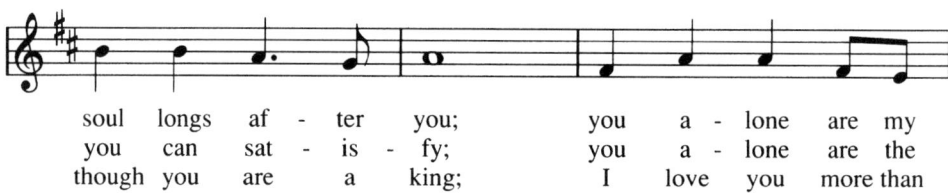

soul longs af-ter you; you a-lone are my
you can sat-is-fy; you a-lone are the
though you are a king; I love you more than

heart's de-sire and I long to wor-ship you.
real joy-giv-er and the ap-ple of my eye.
an-y oth-er, so much more than an-y-thing!

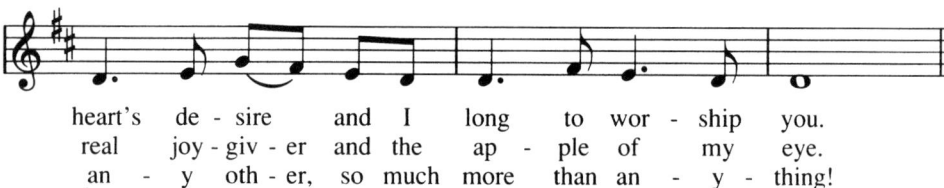

You a-lone are my strength, my shield, to

you a-lone may my spir-it yield; you a-lone are my

heart's de-sire, and I long to wor-ship you!

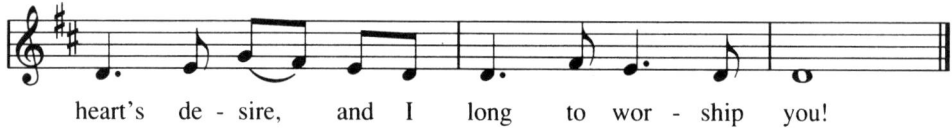

WORDS and MUSIC: Martin Nystrom
© 1984 MARANATHA! MUSIC (Administered by THE COPYRIGHT COMPANY, Nashville, TN)
All Rights Reserved. International Copyright Secured. Used By Permission.

SONGS FOR COMING TO WORSHIP

Be Still and Know 10

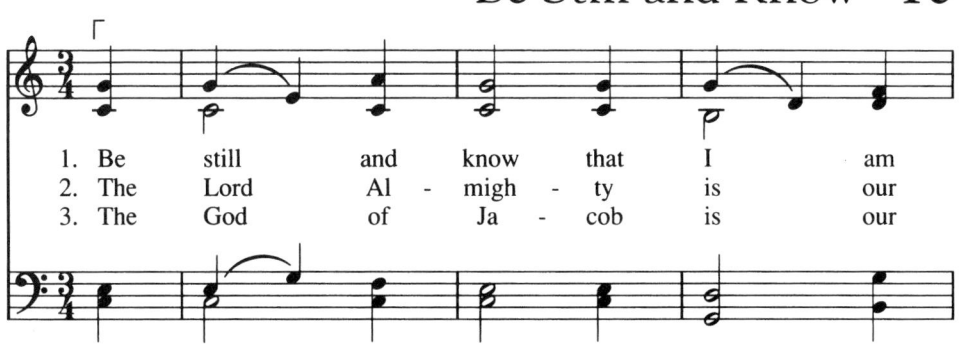
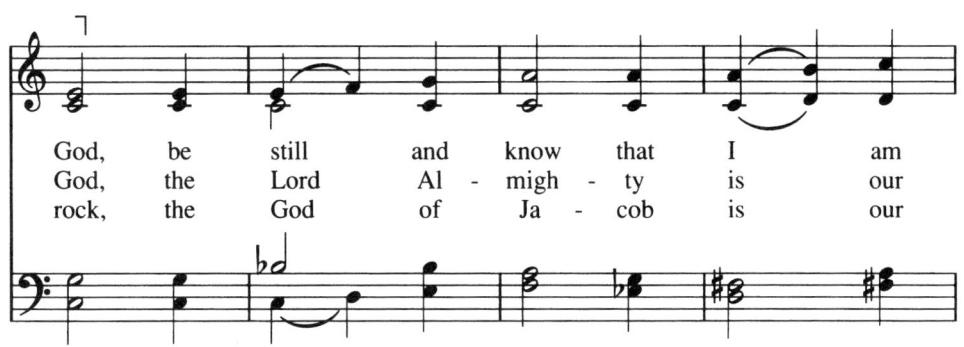
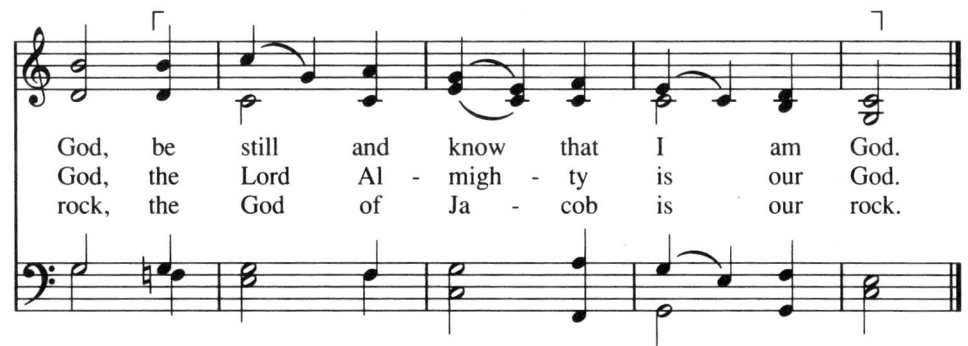

WORDS: Anonymous; para. of Psalm 46:10, 7:1, Exodus 15:26
MUSIC: Anonymous; arr. Jack Schrader, 1988
Music © 1989 Hope Publishing Company

BE STILL AND KNOW
8.8.8.

THE GATHERING

11 Cantemos al Señor
Unisono (Unison)

1. Can - te - mos al Se - ñor   un him - no de a - le -
(2.) te - mos al Se - ñor   un him - no de a - la -
1. Let's sing un - to the Lord   a hymn of glad re -
(2.) sing un - to the Lord   a hymn of ad - o -

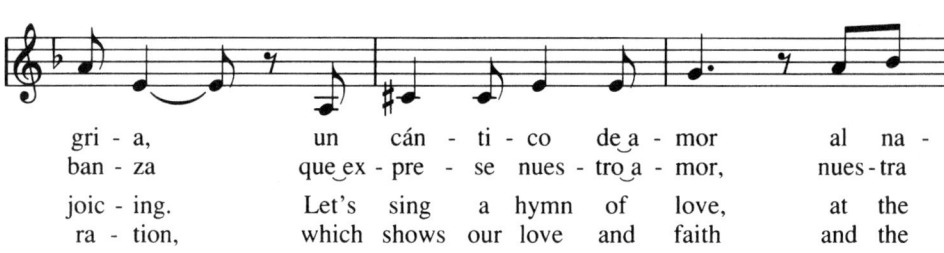

gri - a,   un cán - ti - co de a - mor   al na -
ban - za   que ex - pre - se nues - tro a - mor,   nues - tra
joic - ing.   Let's sing a hymn of love,   at the
ra - tion,   which shows our love and faith   and the

cer el nue - vo dí - a.   Él hi - zo el cie - lo, el
fe y nues-tra es - pe - ran - za. En to - da la crea -
new day's fresh be - gin - ning. God made the sky a -
hope of all cre - at - ion. Through all that has been

mar,   el sol y las es - tre - llas   y
ción   pre - go - na su gran - de - za,   a -
bove,   the stars, the sun, the o - ceans;   and
made,   the Lord is praised for great - ness,   and

WORDS: Carlos Rosas; trans. by Roberto Escamilla, Elise S. Eslinger, and George Lockwood, 1983, 1987 (Ps. 19)
MUSIC: Carlos Rosas; arr. by Raquel Mora Martinez
© 1976 by Resource Publications, 160 E. Virginia Street, #290, San Jose, CA 95112.
Trans. © 1989 The United Methodist Publishing House; arr. © 1983 The United Methodist Publishing House.

ROSAS
67.68 D with Refrain

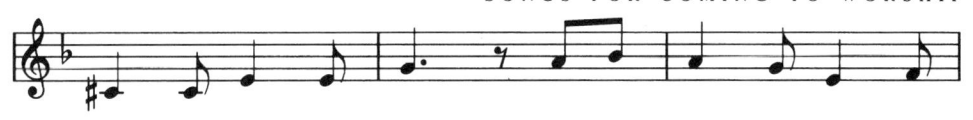

THE GATHERING

12 In the Presence of Your People

WORDS: Psalm 22:3, 22; 145:7; para. Brent Chambers, 1977
MUSIC: Brent Chambers, 1977
© 1977 SCRIPTURE IN SONG, DIV. INTEGRITY MUSIC (Administered by THE COPYRIGHT COMPANY, Nashville, TN) All Rights Reserved. International Copyright Secured. Used by Permission.

CELEBRATION
Irregular

THE GATHERING

14 Here in This Place

1. Here in this place new light is stream-ing,
2. We are the young, our lives are a mys-t'ry,
3. Here we will take the wine and the wa-ter,
4. Not in the dark of build-ings con-fin-ing,

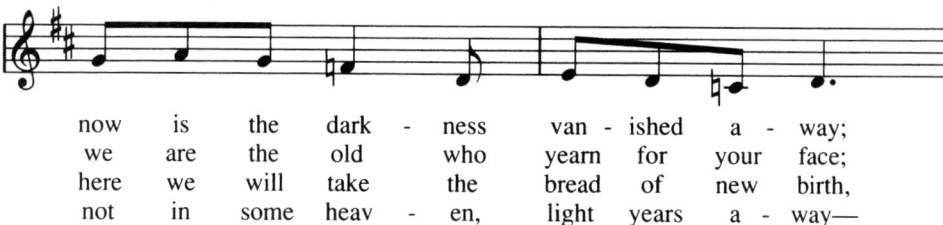

now is the dark-ness van-ished a-way;
we are the old who yearn for your face;
here we will take the bread of new birth,
not in some heav-en, light years a-way—

see in this space our fears and our dream-ings
we have been sung through-out all of his-t'ry,
here you shall call your sons and your daugh-ters,
here in this place the new light is shin-ing,

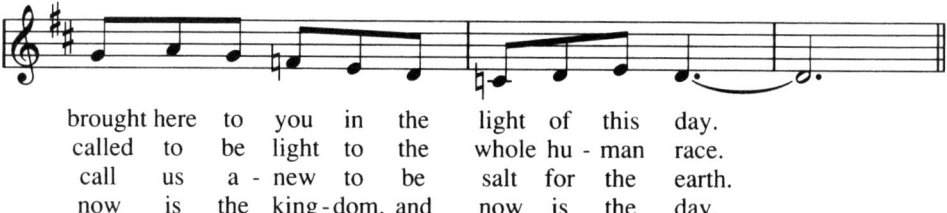

brought here to you in the light of this day.
called to be light to the whole hu-man race.
call us a-new to be salt for the earth.
now is the king-dom, and now is the day,

TEXT: Marty Haugen
MUSIC: Marty Haugen
© 1982 by G.I.A. Publications, Inc., Chicago, Illinois.
All Rights Reserved. Used by Permission.

SONGS FOR COMING TO WORSHIP

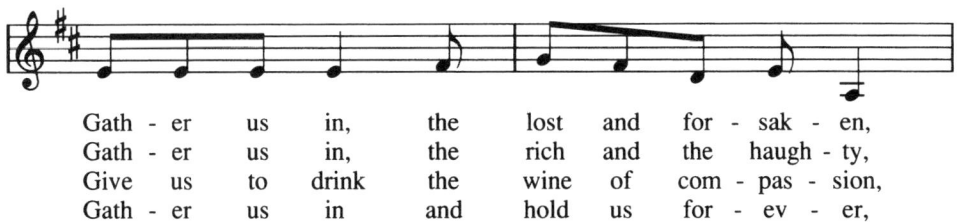

Gath - er us in, the lost and for - sak - en,
Gath - er us in, the rich and the haugh - ty,
Give us to drink the wine of com - pas - sion,
Gath - er us in and hold us for - ev - er,

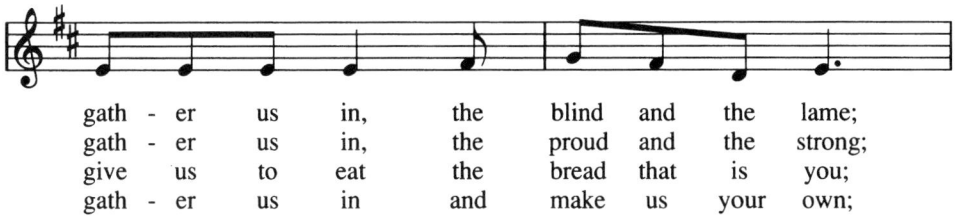

gath - er us in, the blind and the lame;
gath - er us in, the proud and the strong;
give us to eat the bread that is you;
gath - er us in and make us your own;

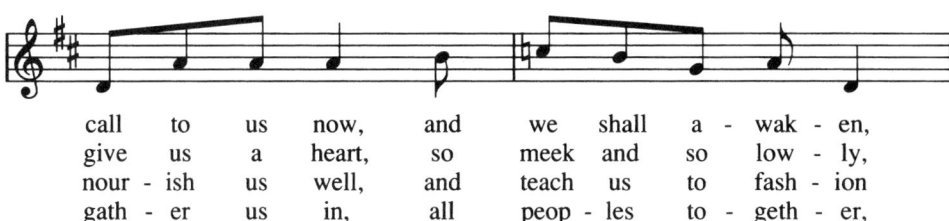

call to us now, and we shall a - wak - en,
give us a heart, so meek and so low - ly,
nour - ish us well, and teach us to fash - ion
gath - er us in, all peop - les to - geth - er,

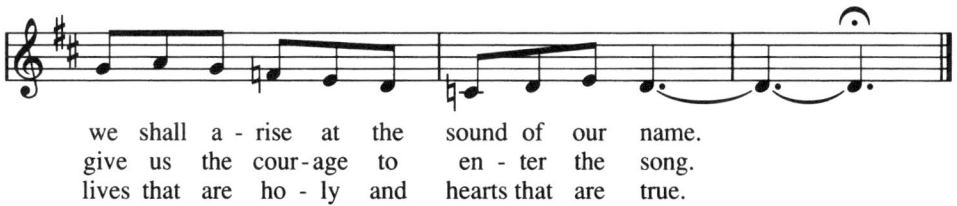

we shall a - rise at the sound of our name.
give us the cour - age to en - ter the song.
lives that are ho - ly and hearts that are true.
fire____ of love in our flesh and our bone.

THE GATHERING

15 I Will Call Upon the Lord

WORDS: adapted from Psalm 18 by Michael O'Shields
MUSIC: Michael O'Shields
Copyright © 1979 by Sound III and All Nations Music.
All Rights Reserved. Used by Permission.

SONGS FOR COMING TO WORSHIP

THE GATHERING

16 Bless His Holy Name

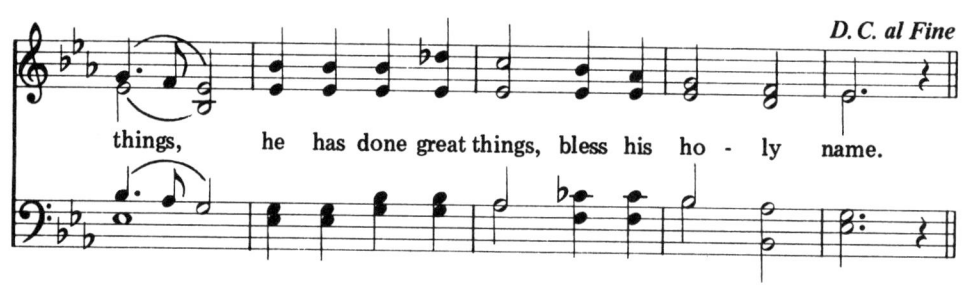

WORDS and MUSIC: Andraé Crouch, 1973; based on Psalm 103:1
© 1973 Bud John Songs, Inc. Admin. by EMI Christian Music Publishing.
All Rights Reserved. Used by Permission.

BLESS HIS HOLY NAME
Irregular

SONGS FOR COMING TO WORSHIP

Jesus, Stand Among Us 17

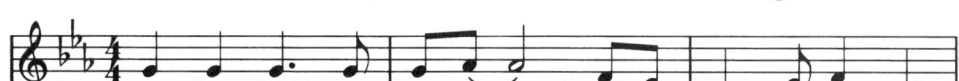

1. Je - sus, stand a - mong us at the meet - ing of our
2. So to You we're gath - er - ing out of each and ev - ery
3. Je - sus, stand a - mong us at the break - ing of the

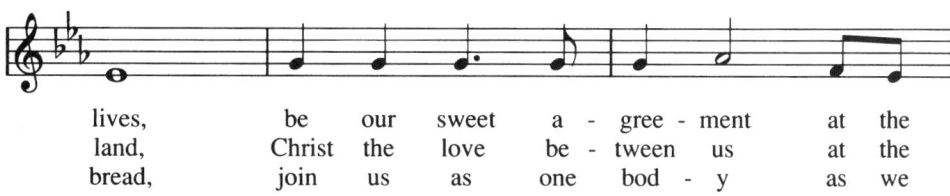

lives, be our sweet a - gree - ment at the
land, Christ the love be - tween us at the
bread, join us as one bod - y as we

meet - ing of our eyes; O, Je - sus, we love You,
join - ing of our hands; O, Je - sus, we love You,
wor - ship You, our Head. O, Je - sus, we love You,

so we gath - er here, join our hearts in un - i - ty and

Repeat Ending | Final Ending

take a - way our fear. our fear.

WORDS and MUSIC: Graham Kendrick
© 1977 by Kingsway's Thankyou Music/Adm. in N., S., & C., America by Integrity's Hosanna! Music.
c/o Integrity Music, Inc., P.O. Box 851622, Mobile, AL 36685.
All Rights Reserved. International Copyright Secured. Used by Permission.

THE GATHERING

18 Come, Let Us with Our Lord Arise

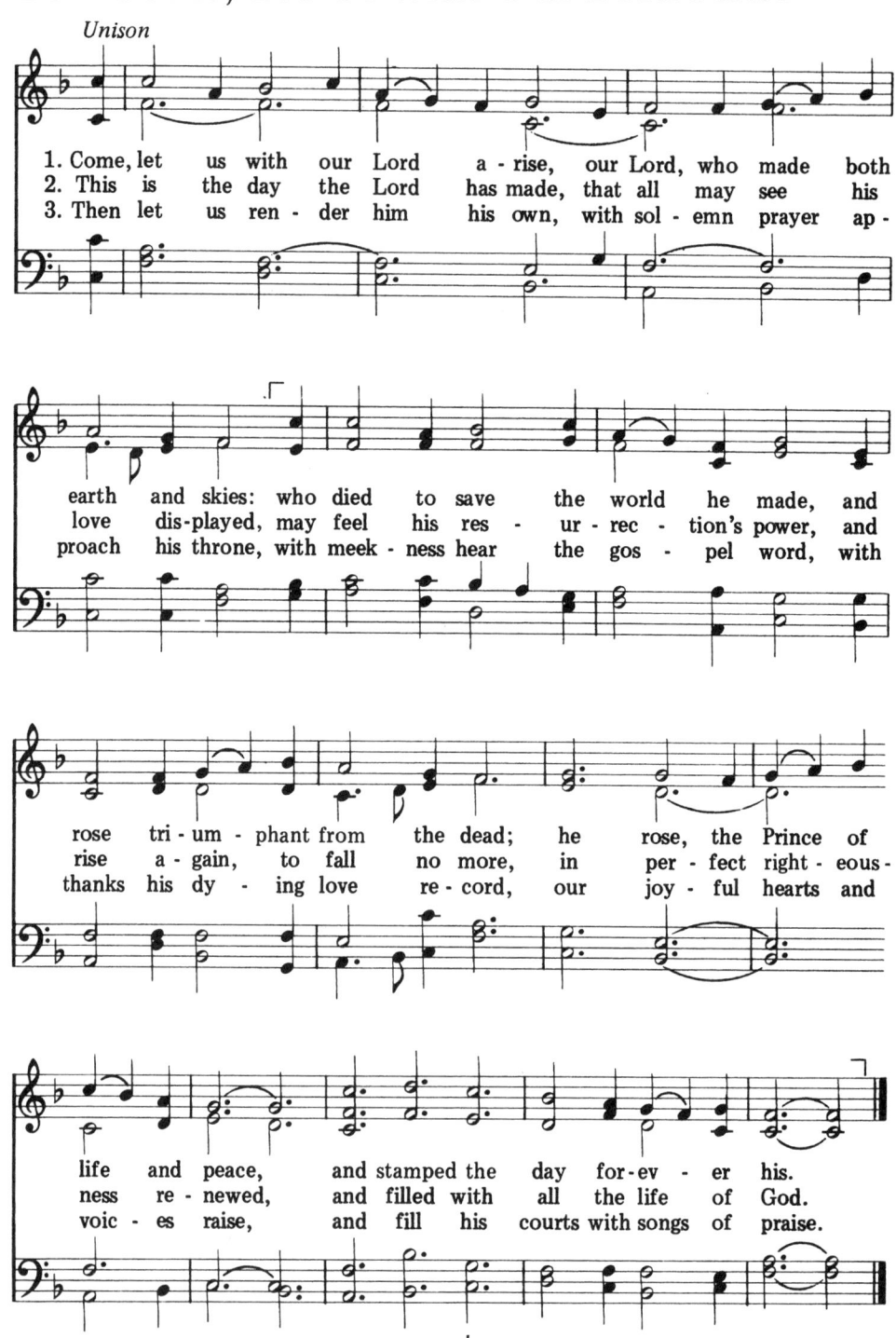

1. Come, let us with our Lord arise, our Lord, who made both earth and skies: who died to save the world he made, and rose triumphant from the dead; he rose, the Prince of life and peace, and stamped the day forever his.
2. This is the day the Lord has made, that all may see his love displayed, may feel his resurrection's power, and rise again, to fall no more, in perfect righteousness renewed, and filled with all the life of God.
3. Then let us render him his own, with solemn prayer approach his throne, with meekness hear the gospel word, with thanks his dying love record, our joyful hearts and voices raise, and fill his courts with songs of praise.

WORDS: Charles Wesley, 1763
MUSIC: Traditional English melody; harm. Ralph Vaughan Williams, 1919
Music © 1919 Stainer & Bell Ltd. Used by permission of Hope Publishing Co.

SUSSEX CAROL
8.8.8.8.8.8.

THE GATHERING

20 Come and Rejoice

Verse
♩. = 54

1. Come with re-joic-ing, the Fa-ther is call-ing,
2. Lord of cre-a-tion is full of com-pas-sion,
3. sound of the trum-pet he sum-mons the na-tions,

those who would wor-ship in spir-it and truth;
seat-ed in splen-dor a-dorned with all grace; ma-
call-ing a priest-hood to go in His name; to

Come with your sing-ing, come with thanks-giv-ing,
jes-tic and glo-rious, reign-ing vic-tor-ious,
show forth His pow-er to this gen-er-a-tion, to

Je-sus, our Sav-ior, has made all things new.
now and for-ev-er en-throned on our praise.
wor-ship be-fore him, a king-dom of praise.

Chorus

Come and re-joice, O ho-ly na-tion, come and sing prais-es to him;

come and bow down, wor-ship be-fore him, Je-sus, the King of all

|1, 2| |3 *Fine*|

kings, Je-sus, the King of all kings. The kings.
With the

WORDS and MUSIC: Don Moen and Gerrit Gustafson
© 1989 Integrity's Hosanna! Music
c/o Integrity Music, Inc., P.O. Box 851622, Mobile, AL 36685.
All Rights Reserved. International Copyright Secured. Used by Permission

SONGS FOR COMING TO WORSHIP

Sing a New Song 21

Sing a new song un-to the Lord; let your song be

sung from moun-tains high. Sing a new song

un-to the Lord, sing-ing, "Al - le - lu - ia."

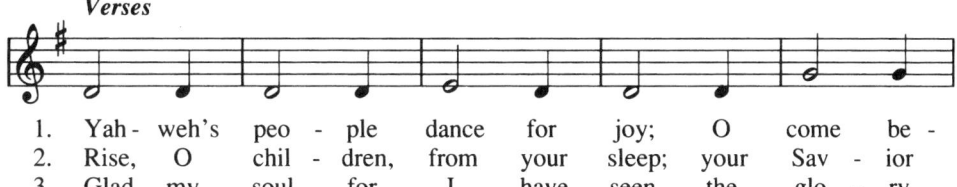

1. Yah - weh's peo - ple dance for joy; O come be -
2. Rise, O chil - dren, from your sleep; your Sav - ior
3. Glad my soul for I have seen the glo - ry

fore the Lord. And play for him on
now has come. He has turned your
of the Lord. The trum - pet sounds; the

To Refrain

glad tam - bou - rines, and let your trum - pet sound.
sor - row to joy, and filled your soul with song.
dead shall be raised. I know my Sav - ior lives.

WORDS and MUSIC: Daniel L. Schutte
© 1972, 1974, Daniel L. Schutte. Administered by New Dawn Music,
5536 NE Hassalo, Portland, OR 97213.
All Rights Reserved. Used by Permission.

Songs About God

22 Great Is the Lord

Great is the Lord, he is ho-ly and just; by his pow-er we trust in his love.

Great is the Lord, he is faith-ful and true; by his mer-cy he proves he is love.

Harmony

1, 2. Great is the Lord and wor-thy of glo-ry! Great is the Lord and
D.S. *Great are you, Lord, and wor-thy of glo-ry! Great are you, Lord, and*

wor-thy of praise. Great is the Lord; now lift up your voice, now lift up your voice:
wor-thy of praise. Great are you, Lord; I lift up my voice, I lift up my voice:

WORDS and MUSIC: Michael W. Smith and Deborah D. Smith, 1982
© 1982 Meadowgreen Music Company. Admin. by EMI Christian Music Publishing.
All Rights Reserved. Used with Permission.

GREAT IS THE LORD
Irregular

SONGS ABOUT GOD

The Steadfast Love of the Lord 23

The stead-fast love of the Lord nev-er ceas-es, his mer-cies nev-er come to an end. They are new ev-'ry morn-ing, new ev-'ry morn-ing, great is your faith-ful-ness, O Lord, great is your faith-ful-ness, O Lord, great is your faith-ful-ness.

WORDS and MUSIC: Edith McNeill
© 1974 CELEBRATION (Administered by THE COPYRIGHT COMPANY, Nashville, TN)
All Rights Reserved. International Copyright Secured. Used by Permission.

THE GATHERING

24 Jehovah-Jireh

WORDS and MUSIC: Merla Watson
Copyright © 1974 & 1994 by Sound III and All Nations Music.
Used by permission. All rights reserved.

SONGS ABOUT GOD

You Have Been Good 25

WORDS and MUSIC: Twila Paris
© 1988 Ariose Music/Mountain Spring Music
Admin. by EMI Christian Music Publishing.
All Rights Reserved. Reprinted by Permission.

THE GATHERING

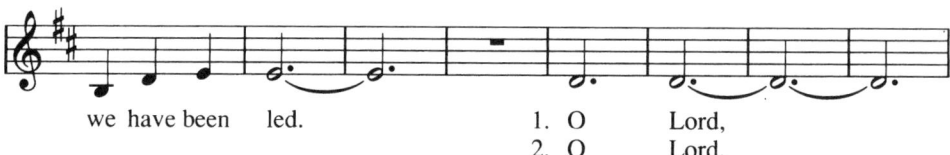

SONGS ABOUT GOD

Jesus, Name Above All Names 26

WORDS and MUSIC: Naida Hearn, 1974
© 1974 SCRIPTURE IN SONG, DIV. INTEGRITY MUSIC (Administered by MARANATHA!
MUSIC c/o THE COPYRIGHT COMPANY, Nashville, TN)
All Rights Reserved. International Copyright Secured. Used by Permission.

HEARN
Irregular

THE GATHERING

27 O How He Loves You and Me!

1. O how he loves you and me, O how he loves you and me; he gave his life—what more could he give? O how he loves you, O how he loves me, O how he loves you and me!

2. Jesus to Cal-v'ry did go, his love for sinners to show. What he did there brought hope from des-pair. O how he loves you, O how he loves me, O how he loves you and me!

WORDS and MUSIC: Kurt Kaiser, 1975
© 1975 Word Music (A Div. of Word, Inc.)
All Rights Reserved. Used by Permission.

PATRICIA
Irregular

28 Emmanuel

Em-man-u-el, Em-man-u-el, his name is called Em-man-u-el.

WORDS and MUSIC: Bob McGee
© 1976 C.A. Music (div. of Christian Artists Corp.)
All Rights Reserved. Used by Permission.

SONGS ABOUT GOD

God with us, reveal'd in us,

his name is called Emmanuel.

He Is Lord 29

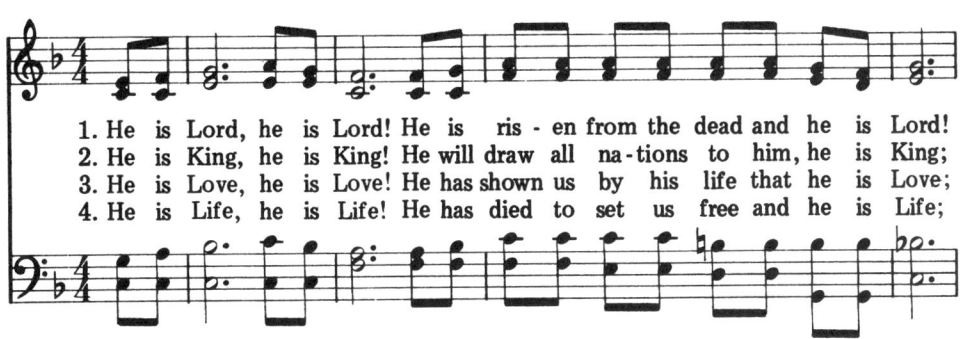

1. He is Lord, he is Lord! He is risen from the dead and he is Lord!
2. He is King, he is King! He will draw all nations to him, he is King;
3. He is Love, he is Love! He has shown us by his life that he is Love;
4. He is Life, he is Life! He has died to set us free and he is Life;

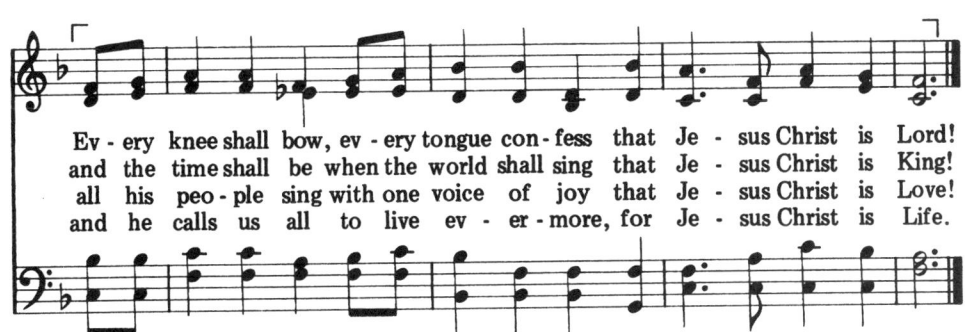

Every knee shall bow, every tongue confess that Jesus Christ is Lord!
and the time shall be when the world shall sing that Jesus Christ is King!
all his people sing with one voice of joy that Jesus Christ is Love!
and he calls us all to live evermore, for Jesus Christ is Life.

WORDS: Anonymous; based on Philippians 2:10-11
MUSIC: Anonymous

HE IS LORD
6.11.10.6.

THE GATHERING

30 His Name Is Wonderful

WORDS and MUSIC: Audrey Mieir, 1959
© Copyright 1959, renewed 1987 by MANNA MUSIC, INC.,
35255 Brooten Road, Pacific City, OR 97135.
All Rights Reserved. Used by Permission.

MIEIR
Irregular

SONGS ABOUT GOD

Righteous One   31

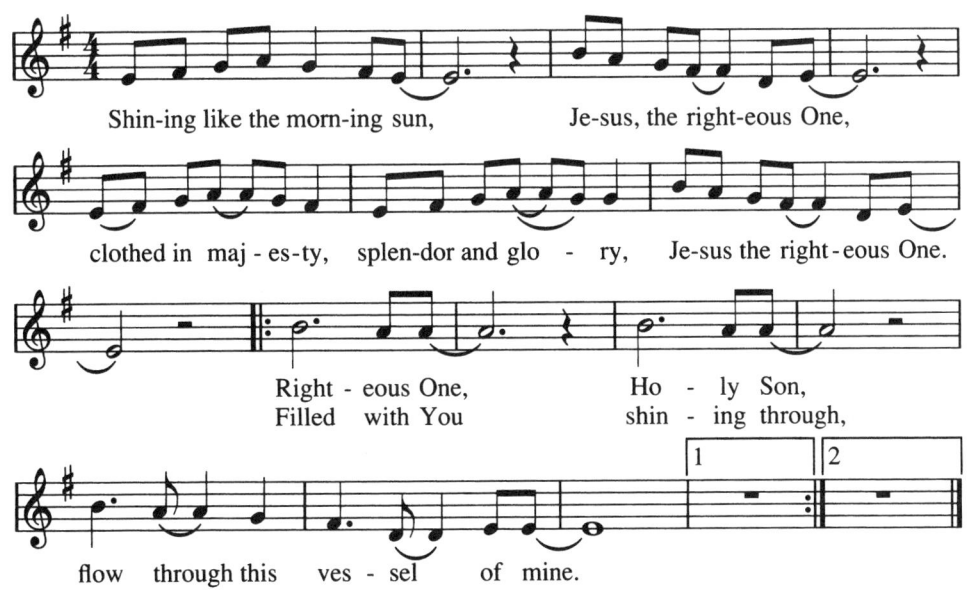

Shining like the morning sun, Jesus, the righteous One,
clothed in majesty, splendor and glory, Jesus the righteous One.
Righteous One, Holy Son,
Filled with You shining through,
flow through this vessel of mine.

WORDS and MUSIC: Bruce Muller and Teresa Muller
© Copyright 1991 MARANATHA! MUSIC (Administered by THE COPYRIGHT COMPANY, Nashville, TN)
All Rights Reserved. International Copyright Secured. Used by Permission.

O for a Thousand Tongues to Sing   32

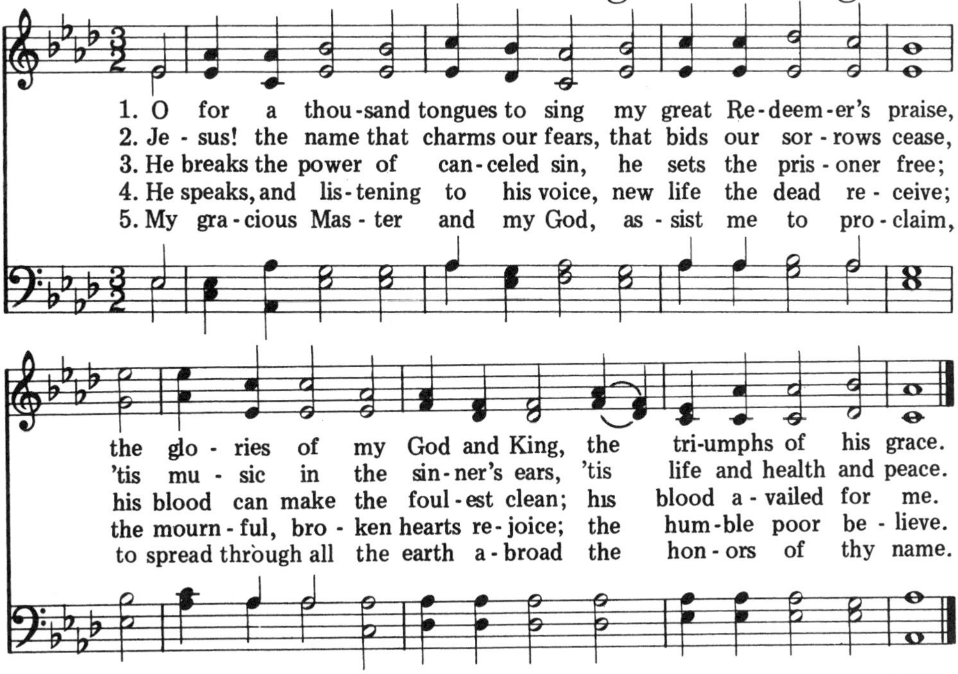

1. O for a thousand tongues to sing my great Redeemer's praise,
   the glories of my God and King, the triumphs of his grace.
2. Jesus! the name that charms our fears, that bids our sorrows cease,
   'tis music in the sinner's ears, 'tis life and health and peace.
3. He breaks the power of canceled sin, he sets the prisoner free;
   his blood can make the foulest clean; his blood availed for me.
4. He speaks, and listening to his voice, new life the dead receive;
   the mournful, broken hearts rejoice; the humble poor believe.
5. My gracious Master and my God, assist me to proclaim,
   to spread through all the earth abroad the honors of thy name.

WORDS: Charles Wesley, 1739
MUSIC: Carl G. Gläser, 1828; arr. Lowell Mason, 1839

AZMON
C.M.

Songs to God

33 We Will Glorify

1. We will glo-ri-fy the King of kings, we will glo-ri-fy the Lamb;
2. Lord Je-ho-vah reigns in maj-es-ty, we will bow be-fore his throne;
3. He is Lord of heav-en, Lord of earth, he is Lord of all who live;
4. Hal-le-lu-jah to the King of kings, hal-le-lu-jah to the Lamb;

we will glo-ri-fy the Lord of lords, who is the great I AM.
we will wor-ship him in right-eous-ness, we will wor-ship him a-lone.
he is Lord a-bove the u-ni-verse, all praise to him we give.
hal-le-lu-jah to the Lord of lords, who is the great I AM.

WORDS and MUSIC: Twila Paris, 1982
Copyright © 1982 Singspiration Music/ASCAP
All Rights Reserved. Used by permission of Benson Music Group, Inc.

WE WILL GLORIFY
9.7.9.6.

THE GATHERING

35 All Hail King Jesus

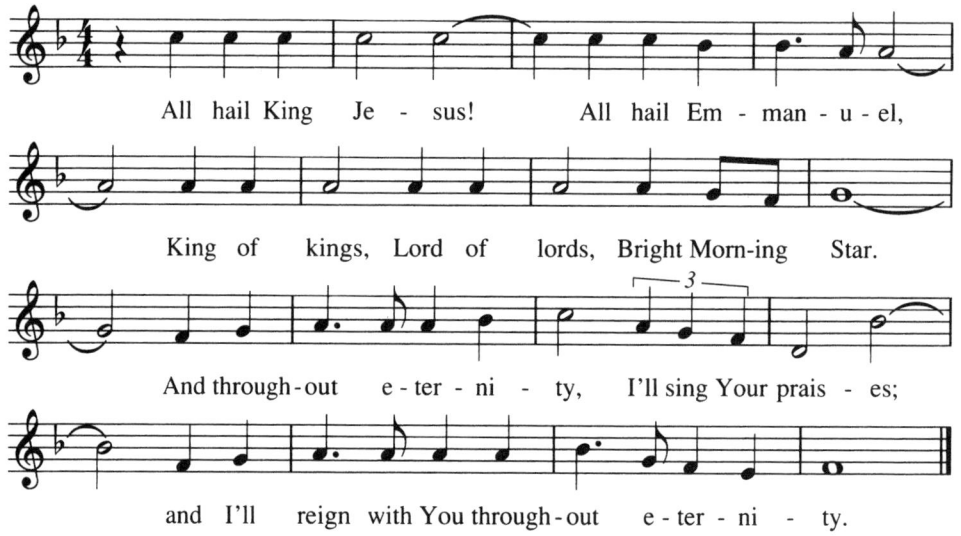

All hail King Jesus! All hail Emmanuel,
King of kings, Lord of lords, Bright Morning Star.
And throughout eternity, I'll sing Your praises;
and I'll reign with You throughout eternity.

WORDS and MUSIC: Dave Moody
Copyright © 1981 Glory Alleluia Music. Administered by Tempo Music Publications, Inc.
All Rights Reserved. Used by Permission.

36 I Love You, Lord

I love you, Lord, and I lift my voice to worship
you, O my soul, rejoice! Take joy, my King, in

WORDS and MUSIC: Laurie Klein, 1978
© 1978 HOUSE OF MERCY MUSIC (Administered by MARANATHA! MUSIC
c/o THE COPYRIGHT COMPANY, Nashville, TN)
All Rights Reserved. International Copyright Secured. Used by Permission.

I LOVE YOU, LORD
9.9.8.10.

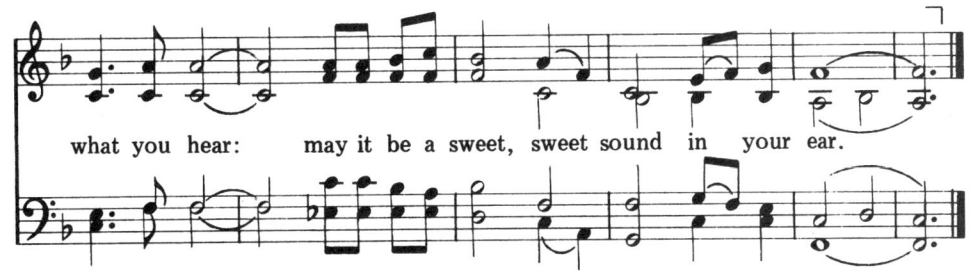

what you hear: may it be a sweet, sweet sound in your ear.

Glorify Your Name 37

1. Fa - ther, we love you, we wor-ship and a-dore you, glo - ri - fy your
2. Je - sus, we love you, we wor-ship and a-dore you, glo - ri - fy your
3. Spir - it, we love you, we wor-ship and a-dore you, glo - ri - fy your

name in all the earth; glo - ri - fy your name, glo - ri - fy your name, glo - ri - fy your name in all the earth.

WORDS and MUSIC: Donna Adkins, 1976
© 1976 MARANATHA! MUSIC (Administered by THE COPYRIGHT COMPANY, Nashville, TN)
All Rights Reserved. International Copyright Secured. Used by Permission.

GLORIFY YOUR NAME
Irregular

SONGS TO GOD

The Highest Place 39

We place You on the high-est place,

for You are the great High Priest.

We place You high a-bove

all else,

and we come to You and

wor-ship at Your feet.

WORDS and MUSIC: Ramon Pink
© 1983 SCRIPTURE IN SONG, DIV. INTEGRITY MUSIC
(Administered by THE COPYRIGHT COMPANY, Nashville, TN)
All Rights Reserved. International Copyright Secured. Used by Permission.

THE GATHERING

40 Lord God, Almighty

Parts

1., 2. Lord God, Almighty, Savior, Redeemer, only true God to be worshipped and praised; how can we tell you how much we love you? Take now our lives, Lord, and teach us to love.

3. Father, we praise you. Jesus, we love you. Spirit, we thank you for the gifts of new life;

2nd time to CODA
(Fine)

Unison

1. "Do not fear for I have redeemed you. You are mine, by name I have called you. When you walk through the waters, I will be there with you.

WORDS and MUSIC: Coni Huisman
© 1984 by Coni Huisman. All RIghts Reserved, Used by Permission.

COMFORT
PM

THE GATHERING

41 When I Look into Your Holiness

WORDS and MUSIC: Wayne & Cathy Perrin
© 1981 Integrity's Hosanna! Music. c/o Integrity Music, Inc.,
P.O. Box 851622, Mobile, AL 36685.
All Rights Reserved. International Copyright Secured. Used by Permission.

SONGS TO GOD

You Are My God 42

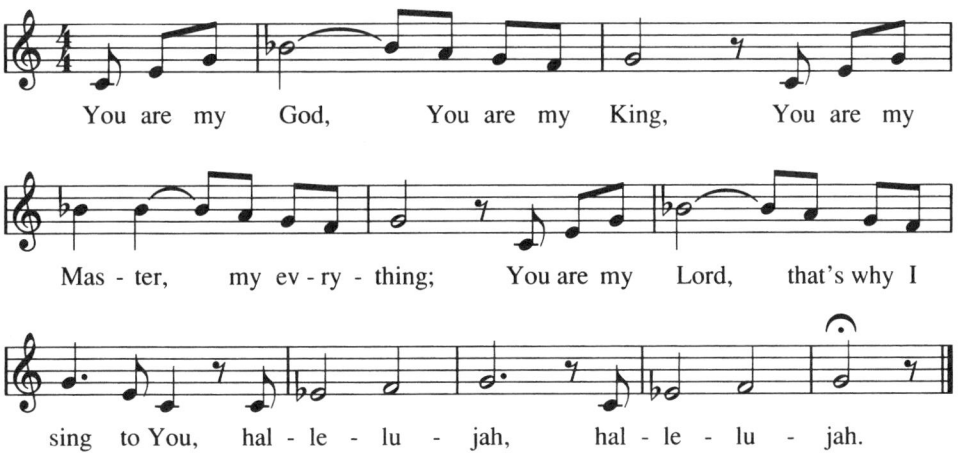

You are my God, You are my King, You are my Master, my ev-ry-thing; You are my Lord, that's why I sing to You, hal-le-lu-jah, hal-le-lu-jah.

WORDS and MUSIC: Macon Delevan
© 1984 Integrity's Hosanna! Music. c/o Integrity Music, Inc.,
P.O. Box 851622, Mobile, AL 36685.
All Rights Reserved. International Copyright Secured. Used by Permission.

Worthy, You Are Worthy 43

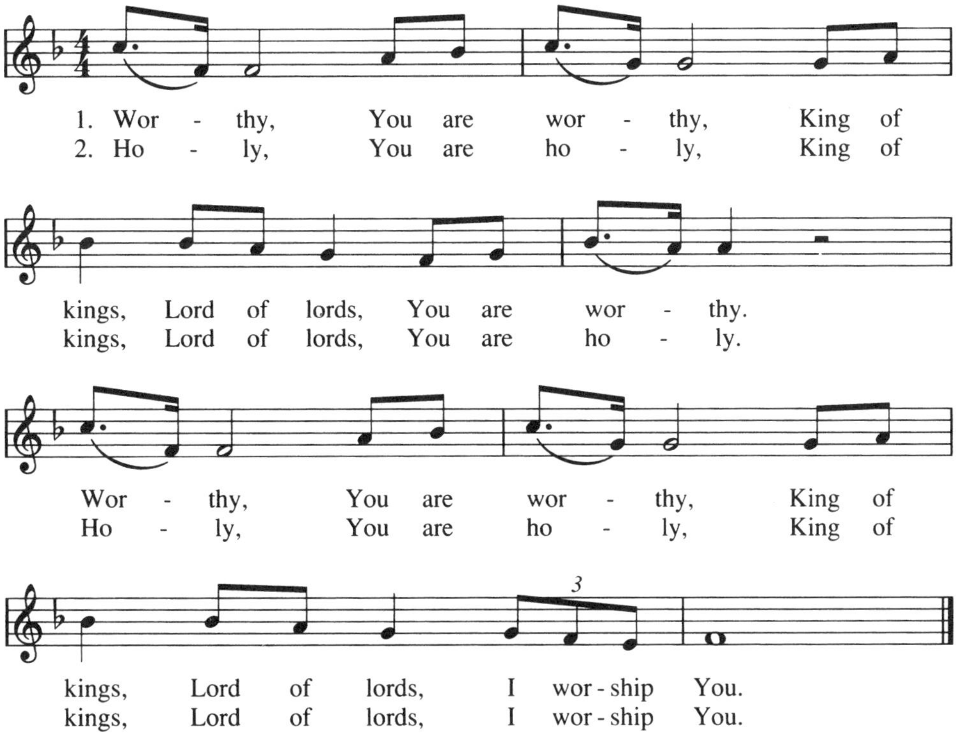

1. Wor-thy, You are wor-thy, King of kings, Lord of lords, You are wor-thy.
   Wor-thy, You are wor-thy, King of kings, Lord of lords, I wor-ship You.
2. Ho-ly, You are ho-ly, King of kings, Lord of lords, You are ho-ly.
   Ho-ly, You are ho-ly, King of kings, Lord of lords, I wor-ship You.

WORDS and MUSIC: Don Moen
© 1986 Integrity's Hosanna! Music. c/o Integrity Music, Inc.,
P.O. Box 851622, Mobile, AL 36685.
All Rights Reserved. International Copyright Secured. Used by Permission.

THE GATHERING

44 I Exalt Thee

For Thou Lord, art high a-bove all the earth.
For You Lord, are high a-bove all the earth.

Thou art ex - al - ted far a - bove all gods.
You are ex - al - ted far a - bove all gods,

for Thou bove all gods. I ex -
for You bove all gods. I ex -

alt Thee I ex - alt Thee I ex - alt Thee
alt You I ex - alt You I ex - alt You

O Lord. I ex - Lord.
O Lord, I ex - Lord.

WORDS and MUSIC: Pete Sanchez, Jr.
Copyright © 1976 by Pete Sanchez, Jr.
All Rights Reserved. International Copyright Secured. Used by Permission.

Processional Hymns

✥ ✥ ✥

All Hail the Power of Jesus' Name 45

1. All hail the power of Je-sus' name! Let an-gels pros-trate fall;
2. Ye cho-sen seed of Is-rael's race, ye ran-somed from the fall,
3. Sin-ners, whose love can ne'er for-get the worm-wood and the gall,
4. Let ev-ery kin-dred, ev-ery tribe, on this ter-res-trial ball,
5. O that with yon-der sa-cred throng we at his feet may fall!

bring forth the roy-al di-a-dem, and crown him Lord of all;
hail him who saves you by his grace, and crown him Lord of all;
go, spread your tro-phies at his feet, and crown him Lord of all;
to him all maj-es-ty as-cribe, and crown him Lord of all;
We'll join the ev-er-last-ing song, and crown him Lord of all;

bring forth the roy-al di-a-dem, and crown him Lord of all!
hail him who saves you by his grace, and crown him Lord of all!
go, spread your tro-phies at his feet, and crown him Lord of all!
to him all maj-es-ty as-cribe, and crown him Lord of all!
we'll join the ev-er-last-ing song, and crown him Lord of all!

WORDS: Edward Perronet, 1780; adapt. John Rippon, 1787
MUSIC: Oliver Holden, 1793

CORONATION
C.M. Repeats

All Creatures of Our God and King 47

WORDS: St. Francis of Assisi, c. 1225; tr. William H. Draper, 1926
MUSIC: *Geistliche Kirchengesäng*, Cologne, 1623; arr. Ralph Vaughan Williams, 1906
Music used by permission of Oxford University Press from the *English Hymnal 1906*.

LASST UNS ERFREUEN
L.M.Alleluias

THE GATHERING

48 Let All Things Now Living

WORDS: Katherine K. Davis, 1939
MUSIC: Traditional Welsh melody; desc. Katherine K. Davis, 1939
© Copyright 1939 (renewed 1966) by E.C. Schirmer Music Company.

ASH GROVE
12.11.12.11.D.

THE GATHERING

49 Let the Whole Creation Cry

1. Let the whole cre-a-tion cry: Alleluia!
   "Glory to the Lord on high!" Alleluia!
   Heaven and earth, awake and sing, Alleluia!
   God is God and therefore King, Alleluia!
2. Praise him, all ye hosts above, Alleluia!
   ever bright and fair in love! Alleluia!
   Sun and moon, lift up your voice; Alleluia!
   night and stars, in God rejoice, Alleluia!
3. Warriors fighting for the Lord, Alleluia!
   prophets burning with his Word, Alleluia!
   those to whom the arts belong, Alleluia!
   add their voices to the song, Alleluia!
4. Men and women, young and old, Alleluia!
   raise the anthem manifold; Alleluia!
   and let children's happy hearts, Alleluia!
   in this worship bear their parts: Alleluia!

WORDS: Stopford A. Brooke, 1881; para. of Psalm 148
MUSIC: Robert Williams, 1817; arr. John Roberts, 1837

LLANFAIR
7.7.7.7.Alleluias

THE GATHERING

51 The God of Abraham Praise

1. The God of Abraham praise, who reigns enthroned above,
Ancient of everlasting days, and God of love.
Jehovah, great I AM, by earth and heaven confessed:
we bow and bless the sacred name forever blest.

2. He by himself hath sworn, we on his oath depend;
we shall, on eagles' wings upborne, to heaven ascend;
we shall behold his face, we shall his power adore,
and sing the wonders of his grace forevermore.

3. The God who reigns on high the great archangels sing,
and "Holy, holy, holy" cry, "Almighty King!
Who was and is the same, and evermore shall be:
eternal Father, great I AM, we worship thee."

4. The whole triumphant host give thanks to God on high;
"Hail, Father, Son and Holy Ghost!" they ever cry.
Hail, Abraham's God and mine! With heaven our songs we raise;
all might and majesty are thine, and endless praise.

WORDS: Thomas Olivers, c. 1770; para. of Hebrew *Yigdal*
MUSIC: Synagogue melody; arr. Meyer Lyon, c. 1770

LEONI
6.6.8.4.D.

PROCESSIONAL HYMNS

Sing Praise to God Who Reigns Above 52

WORDS: Johann J. Schütz, 1675; tr. Frances Cox, 1864, alt.
MUSIC: Bohemian Brethren's *Kirchengesänge*, Berlin, 1566; harm. Heinrich Reimann, 1895

MIT FREUDEN ZART
8.7.8.7.8.8.7.

THE GATHERING

55 The Lord Is Present

WORDS and MUSIC: Gail Cole
Arr. Mimi Farra
© 1975 by Church of the Messiah, 231 E. Grand Blvd., Detroit, MI 48207, U.S.A.
All Rights Reserved. Used by Permission.

PROCESSIONAL HYMNS

Alleluia, Sing to Jesus 58

1. Alleluia, sing to Jesus! his the scepter, his the throne:
Alleluia! his the triumph, his the victory alone.
Hark! the songs of peaceful Zion thunder like a mighty flood.
Jesus, out of every nation, has redeemed us by his blood.

2. Alleluia! not as orphans are we left in sorrow now;
Alleluia! he is near us; faith believes nor questions how.
Though the cloud from sight received him when the forty days were o'er,
shall our hearts forget his promise, "I am with you evermore"?

3. Alleluia! heavenly High Priest, here on earth our help, our stay;
Alleluia! hear the sinful cry to you from day to day.
Intercessor, Friend of sinners, earth's Redeemer, hear our plea,
where the songs of all the sinless sweep across the crystal sea.

WORDS: William C. Dix, 1866, alt.
MUSIC: Rowland H. Prichard, c. 1830; arr. Ralph Vaughan Williams, 1906
Music used by permission of Oxford University Press from the *English Hymnal* 1906.

HYFRYDOL
8.7.8.7.D.

PROCESSIONAL HYMNS

Make Way 60

1. Make way, make way, for Christ the King in splen-dor ar-rives. Fling
2. He comes the bro-ken hearts to heal, the prison-ers to free. The
3. And those who mourn with heav-y hearts, who weep and sigh; with
4. We call you now to wor-ship him as Lord of all, to

wide the gates and wel - come him in - to your lives.
deaf shall hear, the lame shall dance, the blind shall see.
laugh-ter, joy and roy - al crown he'll beau - ti - fy.
have no gods be - fore him— their thrones must fall.

Descant

Make way! Make way! for the King of kings.

Chorus

Make way, make way for the King of kings. Make

Make way! Make way! let his king-dom in.

way, make way and let his king-dom in.

WORDS and MUSIC: Graham Kendrick
© Make Way Music/Adm. in N., S., & C., America by Integrity's Hosanna! Music.
c/o Integrity Music, Inc., P.O. Box 851622, Mobile, AL 36685.
All Rights Reserved. International Copyright Secured. Used by Permission.

THE GATHERING

61 Lift Your Heart to the Lord

Refrain

Lift your heart to the Lord and make this a day of re-joic-ing.

God is our strength and song: glo-ry and praise to his name!

1. Here God's life-giv-ing word once more is pro-claimed to his peo-ple,

Repeat refrain

up-lift-ing those who are down, chal-leng-ing all with its truth.

2. All those bap-tized in-to Christ share the glo-ry of
3. Sum-moned by Je-sus' com-mand, all his peo-ple draw

his res-ur-rec-tion, dy-ing with him un-to
near to his ta-ble, glad-ly to meet with their

Repeat refrain

sin, walk-ing in new-ness of life.
Lord, known in the break-ing of bread.

WORDS: John E. Bowers, 1982, alt., ©
MUSIC: Ralph Vaughan Williams, 1906.
Music used by permission of Oxford University Press from the *English Hymnal 1906*.

SALVE FESTA DIES
Irregular

PROCESSIONAL HYMNS

When in Our Music God Is Glorified 62

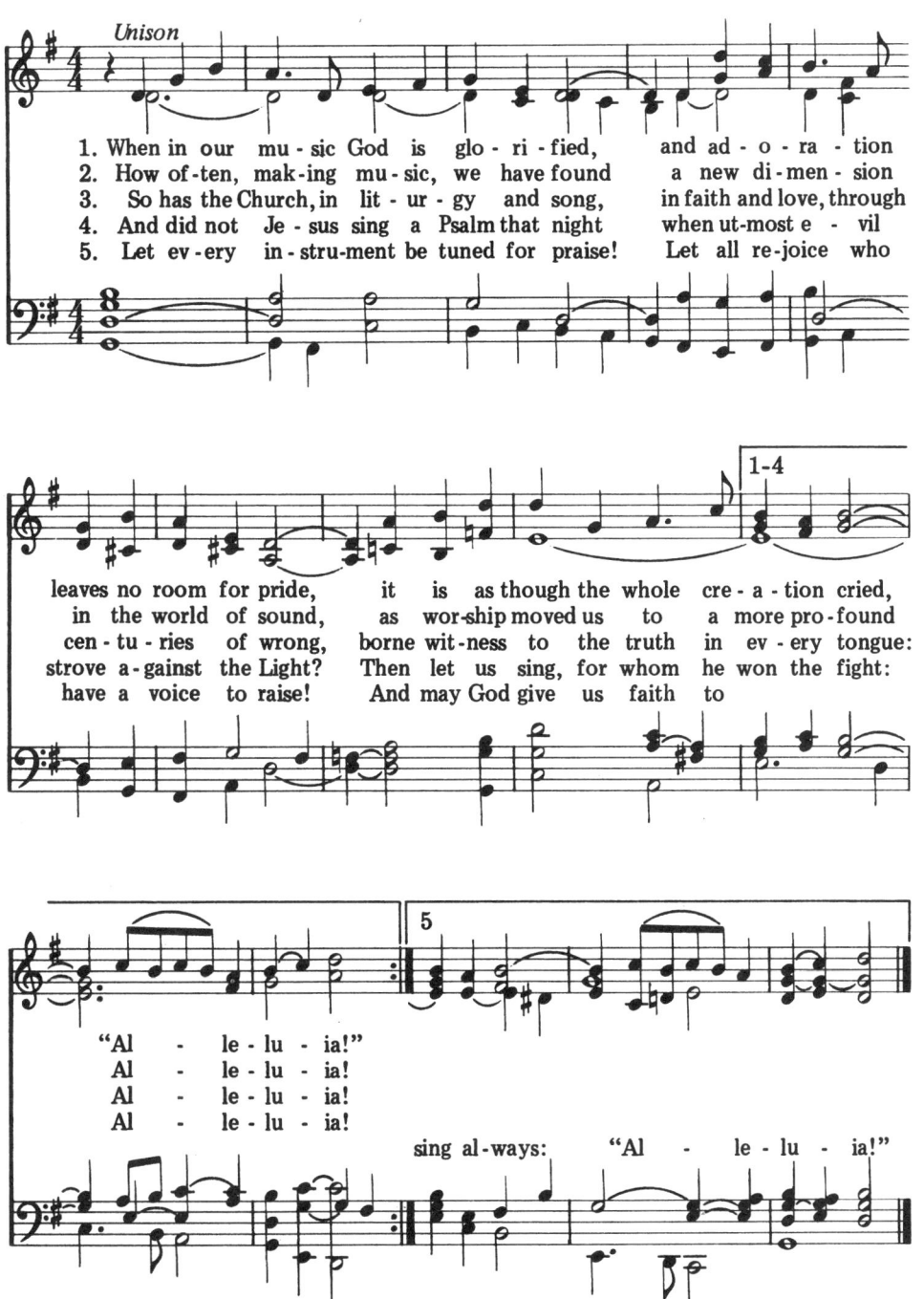

WORDS: Fred Pratt Green, 1971
MUSIC: Charles V. Stanford, 1904
Words © 1972 by Hope Publishing Co., Carol Stream, IL 60188.
All Rights Reserved.

ENGELBERG
10.10.10.Alleluias

Songs of Praise

63 Majesty

WORDS and MUSIC: Jack W. Hayford
© 1981 Rocksmith Music c/o Trust Music Management, Inc.
P.O. Box 9256, Calabasas, California 91372.
Used by Permission. All Rights Reserved.

SONGS OF PRAISE

THE GATHERING

64 Gloria, Gloria

May be sung as a round.

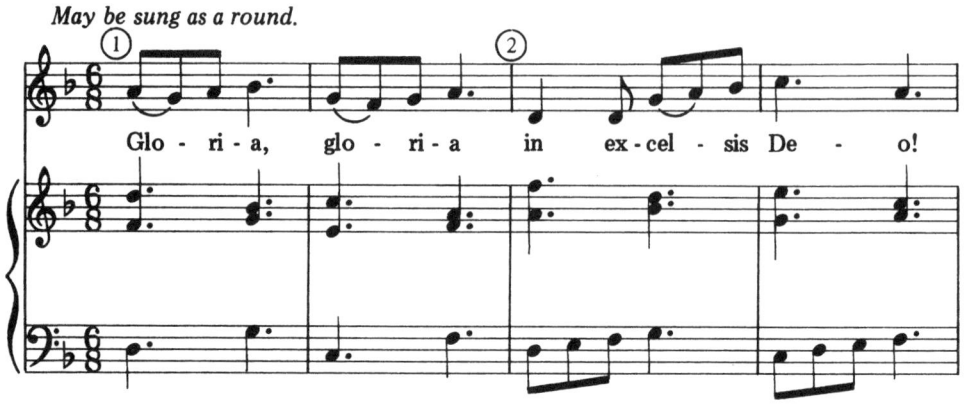

WORDS: Traditional, adapt. Taizé Community, 1978
MUSIC: Jacques Berthier, 1978
Copyright © 1979 by Les Presses de Taizé (France)
Used by permission of G.I.A. Publications, Inc., Chicago, Illinois, exclusive agent.
All Rights Reserved.

GLORIA III
6.6.6.8.

SONGS OF PRAISE

Glory to God, Glory in the Highest 65

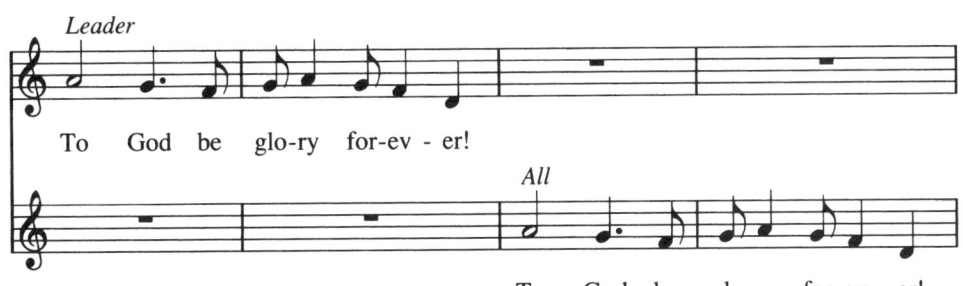

TEXT: Traditional
MUSIC: Lima, Peru, 1982

GLORIA PERU
Irregular

THE GATHERING

66 Glory to God
Gloria in excelsis

Glo-ry to God in the high-est and peace to his peo-ple on earth. Lord God, Heav-en-ly King Al-might-y God our Fa-ther, we wor-ship You; we give You thanks. We praise You for your glo-ry. Glo-ry to God in the high-est and peace to his peo-ple on earth.

Lord Je-sus Christ, the on-ly Son of the Fa-ther, Lord God, Lamb of God, You take a-way the sin of the world; have mer-cy on us.

© 1970, 1971, Daniel L. Schutte. Administered by New Dawn Music
5536 NE Hassalo, Portland, OR 97213
All rights reserved. Used with permission.

THE GATHERING

67 Glory Be to the Father

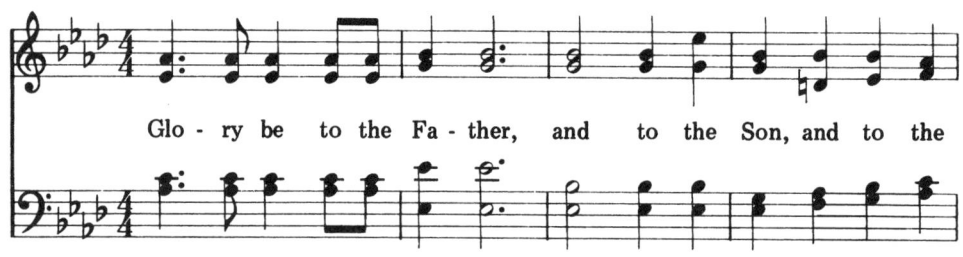

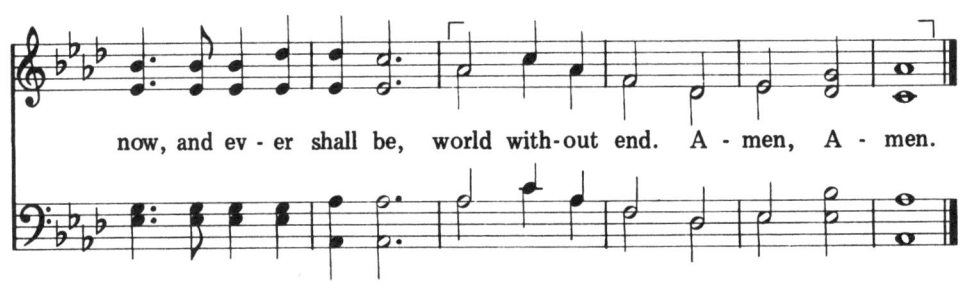

WORDS: *Gloria Patri*, 2nd C.
MUSIC: Christoph Meineke, 1844

MEINEKE
Irregular

SONGS OF PRAISE

My Tribute 68

WORDS and MUSIC: Andraé Crouch, 1971
© 1971 Bud John Songs, Inc. Admin. by EMI Christian Music Publishing.
All Rights Reserved. Used by Permission.

MY TRIBUTE
Irregular

THE GATHERING

69 Great Are You, Lord

Ho - ly Lord, most ho - ly Lord, You a - lone are

wor - thy of my praise; O ho - ly Lord, most

ho - ly Lord, with all of my heart I sing.

Great are You, Lord, great

are You, Lord, great are You,

Lord, great are You, Lord, most ho - ly Lord.

WORDS and MUSIC: Steve Cook and Vikki Cook
© 1984 MARANATH! MUSIC (Administered by THE COPYRIGHT COMPANY, Nashville, TN)
All Rights Reserved. International Copyright Secured. Used by Permission.

THE GATHERING

71 Hosanna

♩ = 120

1. Ho-san-na, Ho-san-na, Ho-san-na in the high-est! Ho-san-na, Ho-san-na, Ho-san-na in the high-est!
2. Glo-ry, Glo-ry, Glo-ry to the King of kings! Glo-ry, Glo-ry, Glo-ry to the King of kings!

Lord we lift up your name with hearts full of praise; Be ex-alt-ed, oh Lord my God! Ho-san-na in the high-est!
Glo-ry to the King of kings!

WORDS and MUSIC: Carl Tuttle
© 1985 Mercy Publishing.

72 Hosanna to the Living King!

Lively

1. I will praise the Lord with harp and string, I will praise the Lord with ev-'ry-thing; I will praise the Lord with all my heart, and
2. I will love the Lord by lov-ing you, I will love the Lord so you'll love him too; I will love the Lord in all I do, for
3. I will give the Lord the things I bear, I will give the Lord my ev-'ry care; for I know his love is al-ways there. His

WORDS and MUSIC: B. Prout and J. Belt
Arr. Betty Pulkingham
© 1976 God Unlimited, Alleluia Community Music, owner,
P.O. Box 6805, Augusta, GA 30916-6805.
All Rights Reserved. Used by Permission.

SONGS OF PRAISE

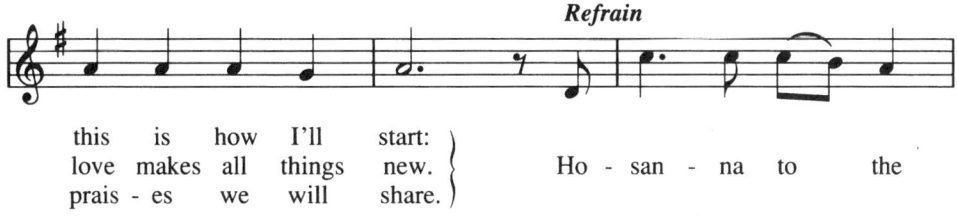

this is how I'll start:
love makes all things new.
prais - es we will share.

Ho - san - na to the

liv - ing King, ho - san - na to the Lord! 'Ho -

san - na,' all cre - a - tion sings to you in one ac - cord.

Lift Up Your Heads 73

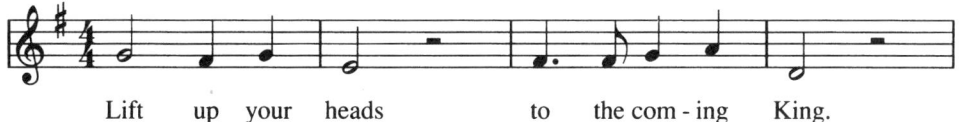

Lift up your heads to the com - ing King.

Bow be - fore Him and a - dore Him, sing

to His Maj - es - ty; let your prais - es be

pure and ho - ly, giv - ing glo - ry to the King of kings.

WORDS and MUSIC: Steven L. Fry
© 1974 Birdwing Music/Cherry Lane Music Publishing Co., Inc.
Admin. by EMI Christian Music Publishing.
All Rights Reserved. Used by Permission.

THE GATHERING

74 Cantad al Señor

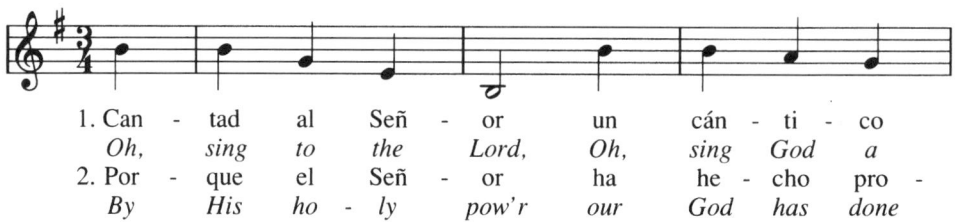

1. Can- tad al Señ - or un cán - ti - co
   Oh, sing to the Lord, Oh, sing God a
2. Por - que el Señ - or ha he - cho pro -
   By His ho - ly pow'r our God has done

nue - vo, can - tad al Señ - or un
new song. Oh, sing to the Lord. Oh,
di - gios por - que el Señ - or ha
won - ders, by His ho - ly pow'r our

cán - ti - co nue - vo, can - tad al Señ -
sing God a new song. Oh, sing to the
he - cho pro - di - gios por - que el Señ -
God has done won - ders. By His ho - ly

or un cán - ti - co nue - vo, ¡can -
Lord, Oh, sing God a new song. Oh,
or ha he - cho pro - di - gios ¡can -
pow'r our God has done won - ders. Oh,

tad al Señ - or, can - tad al Señ - or!
sing to our God. Oh, sing to our God.
tad al Señ - or, can - tad al Señ - or!
sing to our God, Oh, sing to our God.

WORDS: Brazilian folk song; Trans. by Gerhard Cartford. b. 1923, ©
MUSIC: Brazilian folk melody.
Arr. by ISAEC-Editora Sinodal, ©
Trans. © Gerhard Cartford. Used by Permission.

CANTAD AL SEÑOR
Irregular

3. Cantad al Señor,
   alabadle con arpa,
   cantad al Señor,
   alabadle con arpa,
   cantad al Señor,
   alabadle con arpa,
   ¡cantad al Señor,
   cantad al Señor.

4. Es él que nos da
   el Espíritu Santo,
   es él que nos da
   el Espíritu Santo,
   es él que nos da
   el Espíritu Santo,
   ¡cantad al Señor,
   cantad al Señor.

5. ¡Jesús es Señor!
   ¡Amen, aleluya!
   ¡Jesús es Señor!
   ¡Amen, aleluya!
   ¡Jesús es Señor!
   ¡Amen, aleluya!
   ¡cantad al Señor,
   cantad al Señor.

So dance for our God
and blow all the trumpets.
So dance for our God
and blow all the trumpets.
So dance for our God
and blow all the trumpets.
And sing to our God,
and sing to our God.

Oh, shout to our God,
who gave us the Spirit.
Oh, shout to our God,
who gave us the Spirit.
Oh, shout to our God,
who gave us the Spirit.
Oh, sing to our God,
oh, sing to our God.

For Jesus is Lord!
Amen! Alleluia!
For Jesus is Lord!
Amen! Alleluia!
For Jesus is Lord!
Amen! Alleluia!
Oh, sing to our God,
oh, sing to our God.

Praise, I Will Praise You, Lord 76
Je louerai l'Eternel

TEXT: Claude Fraysse, 1976; tr. Kenneth I. Morse. 1988, *Hymnal Sampler*, 1989
Translation copyright © 1989 The Hymnal Project
MUSIC: Alain Bergèse, 1976
© 1976 Alain Bergèse. Translation copyright © 1989 The Hymnal Project, Elgin, IL 60120.

THE GATHERING

77 I Will Celebrate

I will cel-e-brate, sing un-to the Lord;

I will sing to Him a new song.

I will praise Him, for He has tri-umphed vic-

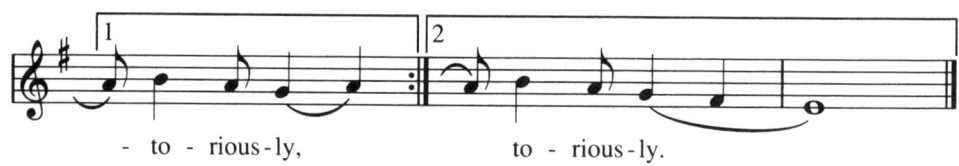

-to-rious-ly,   to-rious-ly.

WORDS and MUSIC: Linda Duvall
© 1982 GRACE FELLOWSHIP (Administered by MARANATHA! MUSIC c/o THE COPYRIGHT COMPANY, Nashville, TN)/
MARANATHA! MUSIC (Administered by THE COPYRIGHT COMPANY, Nashville, TN)
All Rights Reserved. International Copyright Secured. Used by Permission.

78 I Will Exalt My God, My King
Te Exaltaré Mi Dios, Mi Rey

I will ex-alt my God, my King; I will praise Your
Te e-xal-ta-ré, mi Dios, mi Rey, y ben-de-ci-

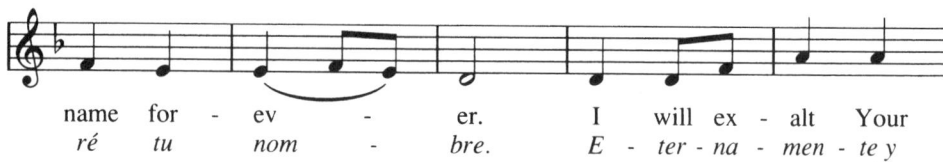

name for-ev-er. I will ex-alt Your
ré tu nom-bre. E-ter-na-men-te y

WORDS: Psalm 145:1–3; vers. Casiodoro Cardenas, 1979; tr. composite
MUSIC: Casiodoro Cardenas, 1979; arr. Raquel Mora Martínez, 1979

ECUADOR
Irregular

SONGS OF PRAISE

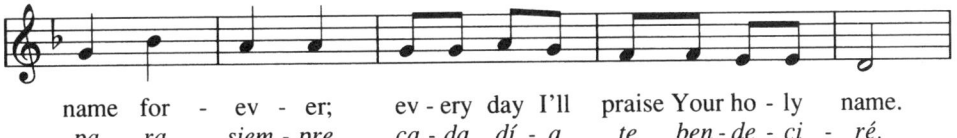
name for - ev - er; ev - ery day I'll praise Your ho - ly name.
pa - ra siem - pre, ca - da dí - a te ben - de - ci - ré.

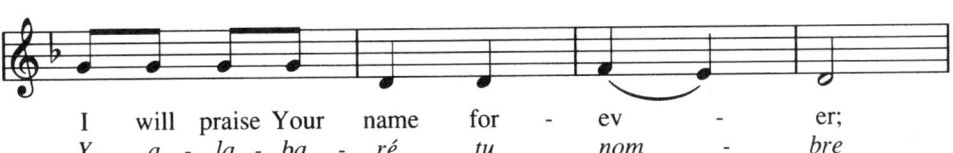
I will praise Your name for - ev - er;
Y a - la - ba - ré tu nom - bre

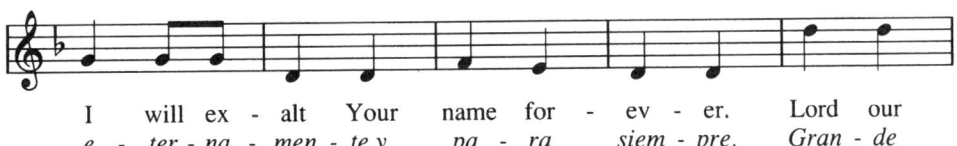
I will ex - alt Your name for - ev - er. Lord our
e - ter - na - men - te y pa - ra siem - pre. Gran - de

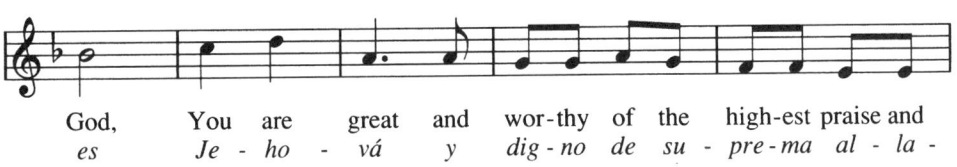
God, You are great and wor-thy of the high-est praise and
es Je - ho - vá y dig - no de su - pre - ma al - la -

hon - or, for Your great-ness is far be-
ban - za; y su gran - de - za es in - es - cru -

yond us; ev - ery day I'll praise Your ho - ly name.
ta - ble; ca - da dí - a te ben - de - ci - ré.

SONGS OF PRAISE

Worthy Is Christ 80
(Digno Es Jesús)

WORDS and MUSIC: Traditional Spanish

DIGNO

THE GATHERING

81 Blessing, Honor and Glory

Bless - ing, hon - or, glo - ry to the

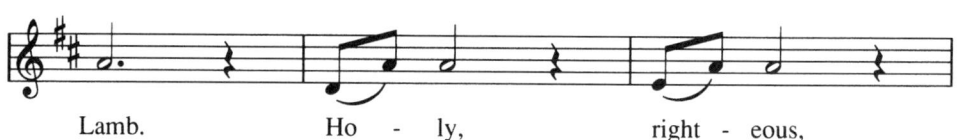
Lamb. Ho - ly, right - eous,

wor - thy is the Lamb. Death could not hold Him down,

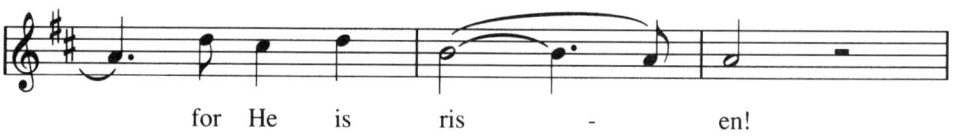
for He is ris - en!

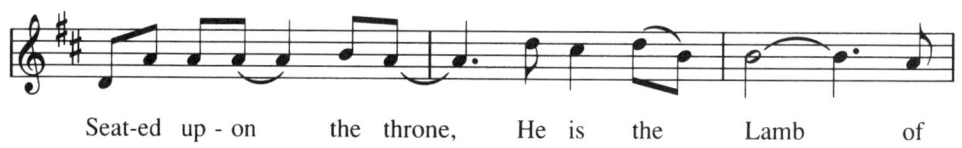
Seat-ed up - on the throne, He is the Lamb of

God! God!

Bless - ing, hon - or, glo - ry to the

WORDS and MUSIC: Geoff Bullock and David Reidy
© 1990 by Nightlight Music (adm. by WORD, INC.)
All Rights Reserved. Used by Permission.

SONGS OF PRAISE

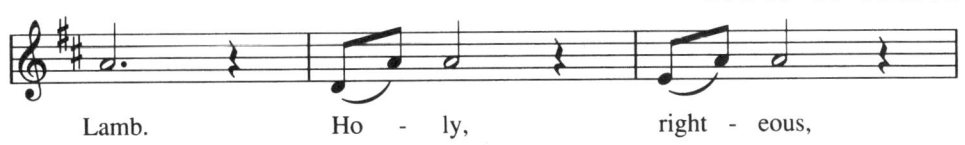
Lamb. Ho - ly, right - eous,

wor - thy is the Lamb of God.

Doxology 82

Praise God from whom all bless - ings flow, praise

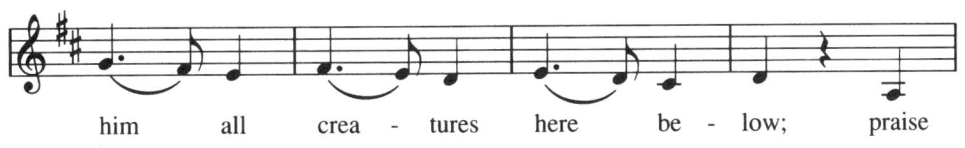
him all crea - tures here be - low; praise

him a - bove, you heav - en - ly host, praise

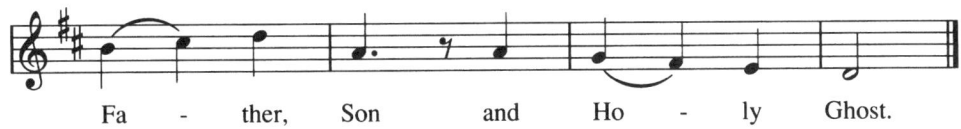
Fa - ther, Son and Ho - ly Ghost.

WORDS and MUSIC: Jimmy Owens
© 1972 Bud John Songs, Inc. Admin. by EMI Christian Music Publishing.
All Rights Reserved. Used by Permission.

83 Praise God from Whom

A Praise God from whom all blessings flow; praise him all creatures here below; praise him above you heav'nly host; praise Father, Son, and Holy Ghost.

B Praise God from whom all blessings flow; in heav'n above and earth below; one God, three persons we adore. To God be praise forevermore. Amen.

SPANISH

A la Divina Trinidad,
todos unido alabad,
con alegria, y gratitud,
su amor y gracia celebrad.

HAUSA

Mai bayarwa ne Allahnmu,
yabe shi, ku 'yan Adam duk.
Yabe shi, ku Mala'iku
uba da Da da Ruhu, daya. Amin.

KOREAN

Manboke keunwon hananim
on bakseong chansong drigo
Jeo cheonsayeo chansonghasei,
chansong seongbu, seogja,
    seongryoung.

CHINESE

Thi^{n}ē bānpang bānkok bānbîn.
Kèng pài Siōngtè, Pē, Kiá^n, Sèng-Sîn.
Oló Samūi itthé Siōngthè.
Chunmiâ liûhoân titkàu bānsè.

TEXT A: Thomas Ken, *A Manual of Prayers for the Use of Scholars in Winchester College*, 1695
TEXT B: after Thomas Ken. Rev. *Hymns for Today's Church*, 1982
  Copyright © 1982 Hope Publishing Co.
MUSIC: Louis Bourgeois, *Genevan Psalter*, 1551

Songs of Confession and Lament

❖ ❖ ❖

Lord Have Mercy 84

Lord have mer - cy,

Christ have mer - cy,

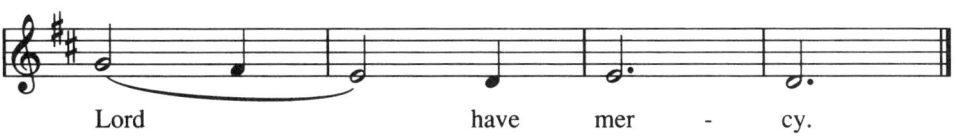

Lord have mer - cy.

WORDS and MUSIC: John Michael Talbot
© 1988 Birdwing Music. Admin. by EMI Christian Music Publishing.
All Rights Reserved. Used by Permission.

THE GATHERING

85 Lord, Have Mercy upon Us

WORDS: *Kyrie eleison*
MUSIC: Healey Willan, 1928
© Oxford University Press 1928. Renewed in USA 1956.

WILLAN KYRIE
Irregular

86 Kyrie Eleison

WORDS: Greek litany
MUSIC: Russian Orthodox liturgy

SONGS OF CONFESSION AND LAMENT

How Long, O Lord 87

Moderately with expression

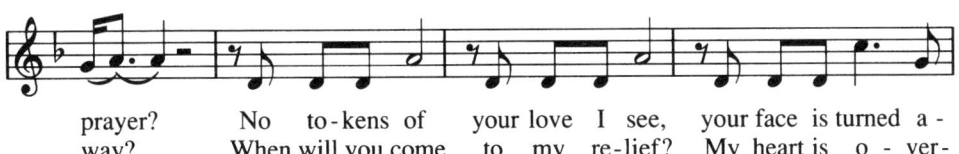

1. How long, O Lord, will you for-get an ans-wer to my
2. How long, O Lord, will you for-sake and leave me in this
3. How long, O Lord but you for-give, with mer-cy from a-

prayer? No to-kens of your love I see, your face is turned a-
way? When will you come to my re-lief? My heart is o-ver-
bove. I find that all your ways are just, I learn to praise you

way from me; I wres-tle with des - pair.
whelmed with grief, by e - vil night and day.
and to trust in your un-fail - ing love.

WORDS: from Psalm 13
MUSIC: Christopher Norton
Words © 1989 by Hope Publishing Co., Carol Stream, IL 60188.
Music © Harper Collins *Publishers* (adm. by CopyCare Ltd.)

By the Waters 88

Canon

(1) By the wa-ters, the wa-ters of Ba-by-lon,

(2) we sat down and wept, and wept for you, Zi-on.

(3) We re-mem-ber you, re-mem-ber you, re-mem-ber you, Zi-on.

WORDS: Based on Psalm 137
MUSIC: Traditional melody

THE GATHERING

89 The City Is Alive, O God

1. The cit-y is a - live, O God, with sound of hus - tling
2. Is it your will, O lov - ing God, that rac - es live in
3. In Gal - i - lee the peo - ple heard your ser - vant Christ de -
4. O God, in - spire your church to-day to take Christ's ser - vant

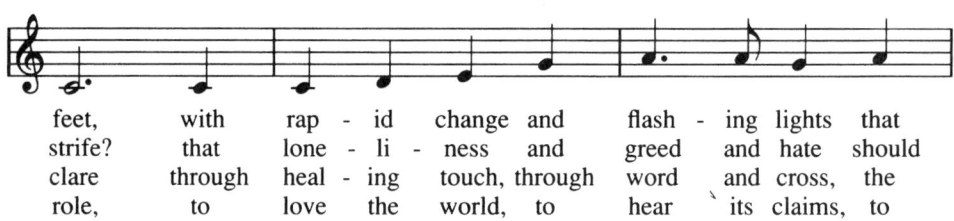

feet, with rap - id change and flash - ing lights that
strife? that lone - li - ness and greed and hate should
clare through heal - ing touch, through word and cross, the
role, to love the world, to hear its claims, to

pulse through ev - ery street; but oft there's in - hu -
mark a cit - y's life? Do you de - sire one
good news of your care. He said your heart touched
sense its yearn - ing soul, to live with - in the

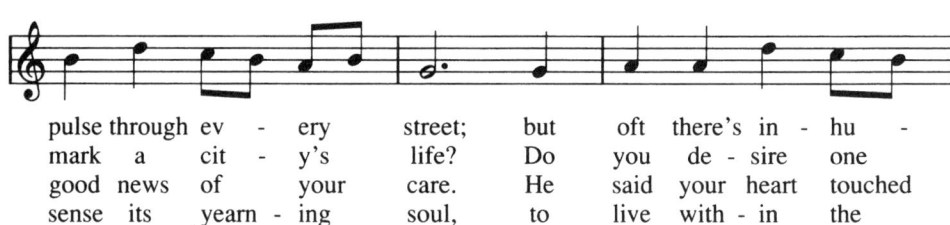

man - i - ty be - hind the bright fa - cade, and
per - son's wealth to keep an - oth - er poor? Must
ev - ery heart that longed for peace and right, that
mar - ket - place, to serve both weak and strong, to

throngs with emp - ty, hun-gering hearts cry out for help, O God.
crime and slums and lust a - bound? O Lord, is there no cure?
those bowed down by bur - dens borne could find your life, your light.
lose it - self, to share its dream, to give the world its song.

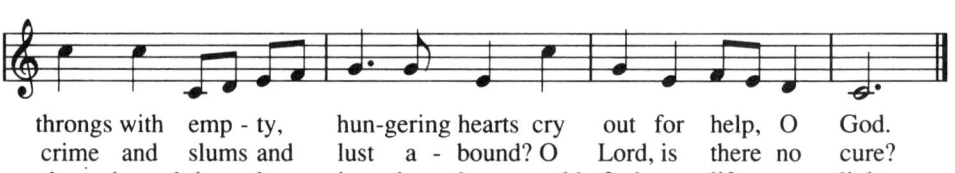

WORDS: William W. Reid, Jr., alt.
MUSIC: Eric H. Thiman, 1923.
Words © 1969 by The Hymn Society (admin. by Hope Publishing Co., Carol Stream, IL 60188) All Rights Reserved.
Music © Novello & Co., Ltd., 8/9 Frith Street, London

The Service of the Word

Songs of Illumination

90 Spirit of the Living God

1. Spir-it of the liv-ing God, fall a-fresh on me.
   fall a-fresh on me. Break me, melt me, mold me, fill me.
   Spir-it of the liv-ing God, fall a-fresh on me.

2. Spir-it of the liv-ing God, move a-mong us all;
   make us one in love: hum-ble, car-ing, self-less, shar-ing—
   Spir-it of the liv-ing God, fill our lives with love!

WORDS: Daniel Iverson, 1926, *Revival Songs*, 1929; St. 2 Michael Baughen
MUSIC: Daniel Iverson, 1926, *Revival Songs*, 1929;
Arranged by Herbert G. Tovey
© 1935, 1963 Birdwing Music. Admin. by EMI Christian Music Publishing.
All Rights Reserved. Used by Permission.
St. 2 © 1982 by Hope Publishing Co.

SONGS OF ILLUMINATION

Open Our Eyes, Lord 91

1. O-pen our eyes, Lord, we want to see Je - sus,
2. O-pen our ears, Lord, and help us to lis - ten,

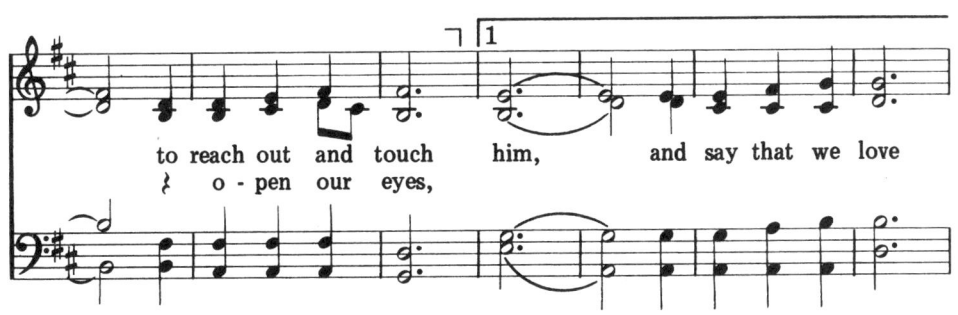

to reach out and touch him, and say that we love
{ o - pen our eyes,

him. Lord, we want to see Je - sus.

WORDS and MUSIC: Robert Cull, 1976; arr. David Allen, 1976
© 1976 MARANATHA! MUSIC (Administered by THE COPYRIGHT COMPANY, Nashville, TN)
All Rights Reserved. International Copyright Secured. Used by Permission.

OPEN OUR EYES
11.12.11.11.

THE SERVICE OF THE WORD

92 Prepare the Way

WORDS: From Scripture
MUSIC: From the Taizé Community
Copyright © Les Presses de Taizé (France). Used by Permission of G.I.A. Publications, Inc.,
Chicago, IL, exclusive agent. All Rights Reserved.

THE SERVICE OF THE WORD

94 Thy Word

Repeat after each verse (Fine)

Thy Word is a lamp un-to my feet and a light un-to my path.

1. When I feel a-fraid, think I've lost my way, still You're there right be-
2. I will not for-get your love for me, and yet my heart for-ev-er is

side me. And noth-ing will I fear as long as You are near.
wan-der-ing. Je-sus, be my guide and hold me to your side; and

D.C.

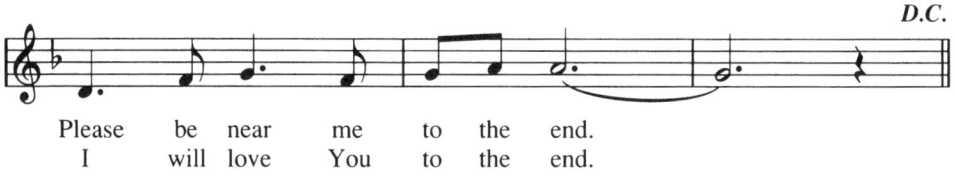

Please be near me to the end.
I will love You to the end.

WORDS and MUSIC: Michael W. Smith and Amy Grant
© 1984 Meadowgreen Music Company/Bug and Bear Music.
Meadowgreen Music Company admin. by EMI Christian Music Publishing.
All Rights Reserved. Used by Permission.

95 Holy Spirit, Mighty God

1. Ho-ly Spir-it, might-y God, tune our ears to
2. Ho-ly Spir-it, might-y God, move our will, de-
3. Ho-ly Spir-it, gra-cious God, source of Sab-bath

WORDS: Calvin Seerveld, 1983, ©
MUSIC: John W. Wilson, 1967.
Words © 1983 Calvin Seerveld, Institute for Christian Studies, Toronto, Ontario, Canada.
Used by Permission.
Music © 1979, Hope Publishing Co., Carol Stream, IL 60188. All Rights Reserved.

LAUDS
77 87

SONGS OF ILLUMINATION

hear the Word; o-pen our hearts, con-vert our lives;
spite our sin, in-to new deeds of truth, not lies;
rest and joy, gen-tle our hurts and still our cries;

mold us strong, sound; make us wise.
teach us love, peace; make us wise.
com-fort, heal, bless; make us wise.

Speak, Lord, in the Stillness 96

1. Speak, Lord, in the still-ness while I wait on Thee;
2. Speak, O bless-ed Mas-ter, in this qui-et hour;
3. For the words You speak, Lord, they are life in-deed;
4. All to You is yield-ed, I am not my own;
5. Fill me with the know-ledge of your glo-rious will;

hushed my heart to lis-ten in ex-pect-an-cy.
let me see your face, Lord, feel your touch of power.
liv-ing bread from heav-en, now my spir-it feed!
bliss-ful, glad sur-ren-der, I am yours a-lone.
all your own good pleas-ure in your child ful-fill.

WORDS: E. May Grimes
MUSIC: Harold Green

Biblical Songs

How Majestic Is Your Name 98
Refrain for Psalms of Creation

WORDS and MUSIC: Michael W. Smith, 1981
© 1981 Meadowgreen Music Co. Admin. by EMI Christian Music Publishing.
All Rights Reserved. Used by Permission.

HOW MAJESTIC
Irregular

THE SERVICE OF THE WORD

99 Sing to the Lord a New Song
Refrain for Psalms of Praise

Sing a new song to the Lord, sing a new song, sing a new song, sing a new song to the Lord.

REFRAIN: Hal H. Hopson, 1984
Music refrain © 1986 by Hope Publishing Co., Carol Stream, IL 60188. All Rights Reserved.

100 A Shield About Me
Refrain for Psalms of Lament

You, O Lord, are a shield a-bout me. You're my glo-ry; You're the lift-er of my head. head. Hal - le - lu - jah,

WORDS and MUSIC: Donn Thomas & Charles Williams
© 1980 by Spoone Music (adm. by WORD, INC.) and Word Music (a div. of WORD, INC.)
All Rights Reserved. Used by Permission.

PSALM REFRAINS

Hail to the Lord's Anointed 101
Refrain for Messianic Psalms

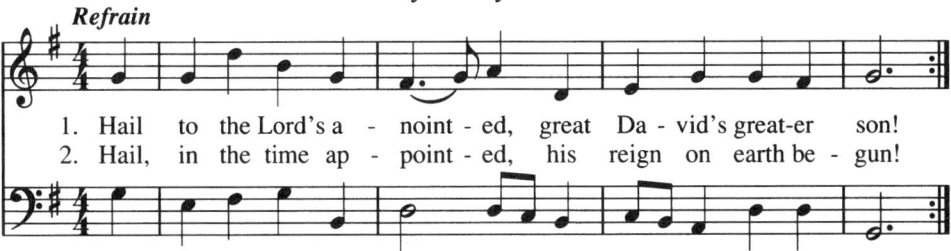

WORDS: From Psalm 72 (NIV); refrain by James Montgomery, 1822
MUSIC: German

The Lord Is My Light 102
Refrain for Psalms of Trust

WORDS: From Psalm 27
MUSIC: From the Taizé Community
Copyright © Les Presses de Taizé (France). Used by permission of G.I.A. Publications, Inc.,
Chicago, IL, exclusive agent. All Rights Reserved.

THE SERVICE OF THE WORD

103 Psalm 1: Planted By the Waters

WORDS and MUSIC: Patsy Hilton Kline
© 1993 by MARANATHA! MUSIC (Administered by THE COPYRIGHT COMPANY, Nashville, TN)
All Rights Reserved. International Copyright Secured. Used by Permission.

SONGS FROM THE PSALMS

Psalm 5: Hear, O Lord, My Urgent Prayer   104

1. Hear, O Lord, my urgent prayer as I come to seek your care. With each morning light I raise voice and heart in prayer and praise.
2. You do not delight in sin or in tales that liars spin. Haughty ones you will defeat with all those who love deceit.
3. By your mercy and your grace I will come before your face. Fearing foes, I bow to pray: lead me, Lord, make straight my way.
4. Save me from deceitful ways; liar's throats are open graves. Make them bear their guilt, O Lord, for by choice they spurn your word.
5. Let those trusting you sing praise; grant them joy to fill their days. Those who always seek the right are protected by your might.

WORDS: Psalm 5; vers. Marie J. Post, 1983
MUSIC: Timothy Hoekman, 1979
Text and music © 1987, CRC Publications, Grand Rapids, MI 49560.
All Rights Reserved. Used by Permission.

TEBBEN
77 77

SONGS FROM THE PSALMS

Psalm 23: The King of Love 106

1. The King of love my shep-herd is, whose good-ness
2. Where streams of liv-ing wa-ter flow my hap-py
3. Though of-ten fool-ish-ly I strayed, still in true
4. In time of death I'll have no fear with You, dear

keeps me ev - er. I want for noth - ing!
soul God leads now, and where the green - est
love God sought me; and told me to be
Lord, be - side me; your rod and staff my

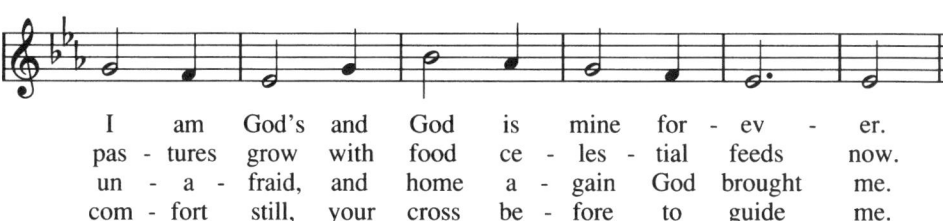

I am God's and God is mine for - ev - er.
pas - tures grow with food ce - les - tial feeds now.
un - a - fraid, and home a - gain God brought me.
com - fort still, your cross be - fore to guide me.

5. You spread a table in my sight,
The bread of life bestowing;
With promise of eternal light
My cup is overflowing!

6. Through all of my remaining days
Then guide me, leave me never,
Good Shepherd, may I sing Your praise
Within Your house forever.

WORDS: Ps 23:1–6
MUSIC: Henry W. Baker, 1821–1877, alt.
Traditional Irish melody

ST. COLUMBA
87 87

THE SERVICE OF THE WORD

107 Psalm 31: 19,20 You Are My Hiding Place

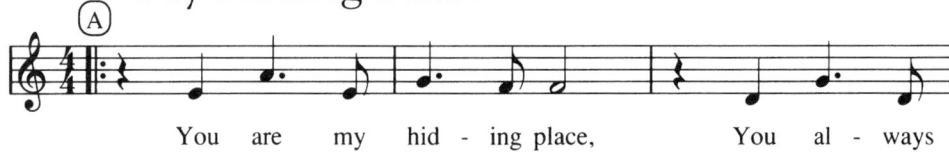

WORDS and MUSIC: Michael Ledner
© 1981 MARANATHA! MUSIC (Administered by THE COPYRIGHT COMPANY, Nashville, TN)
All Rights Reserved. International Copyright Secured. Used by Permission.

SONGS FROM THE PSALMS

Psalm 61: Hear My Cry 108

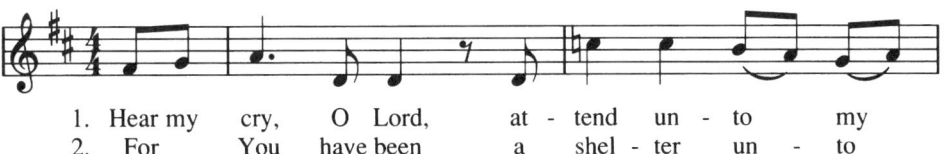
1. Hear my cry, O Lord, at-tend un-to my
2. For You have been a shel-ter un-to

prayer; from the end of the earth will
me, and a strong tow - er

I cry un-to You.
from the en - e - my.
And when my

heart is o - ver-whelmed, please

lead me to the rock that is high-er than I,

that is high - er than I.

Composer Unknown

THE SERVICE OF THE WORD

109 Psalm 63: God Is My Great Desire

1. God is my great desire, his face I seek the first;
to him my heart and soul aspire, for him I thirst.
As one in desert lands, whose very flesh is flame,
in burning love I lift my hands and bless his name.

2. God is my true delight, my richest feast his praise,
through silent watches of the night, through all my days.
To him my spirit clings, on him my soul is cast;
beneath the shadow of his wings he holds me fast.

3. God is my strong defense in every evil hour;
in him I face with confidence the tempter's power.
I trust his mercy sure with truth and triumph crowned:
my hope and joy forevermore in him are found.

WORDS: Psalm 63, para. Timothy Dudley-Smith, 1982
MUSIC: Synagogue melody; arr. Meyer Lyon, 1770
Words © 1984 Hope Publishing Co., Carol Stream, IL 60188. All Rights Reserved.

LEONI
6.6.8.4.D.

THE SERVICE OF THE WORD

111 Psalm 89: I Will Sing of the Mercies

WORDS: Psalm 89:1,5,8; st. 1 vers. James H. Fillmore, 20th C., alt.; st. 2 vers. Marie J. Post, 1983
MUSIC: James H. Fillmore, 20th C.

FILLMORE
Irregular

SONGS FROM THE PSALMS

faith-ful-ness; with my mouth will I make known your faith-ful-ness to
faith-ful-ness? Who can be com-pared to God in faith-ful-ness to

all gen-er-a - tions. I will sing of the mer-cies of the
all gen-er-a - tions? I will sing of the mer-cies of the

Lord for-ev-er, I will sing of the mer-cies of the Lord.
Lord for-ev-er, I will sing of the mer-cies of the Lord.

THE SERVICE OF THE WORD

112 Psalm 91: On Eagle's Wings

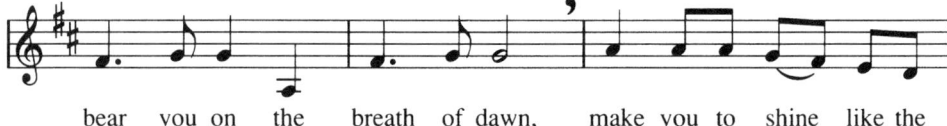

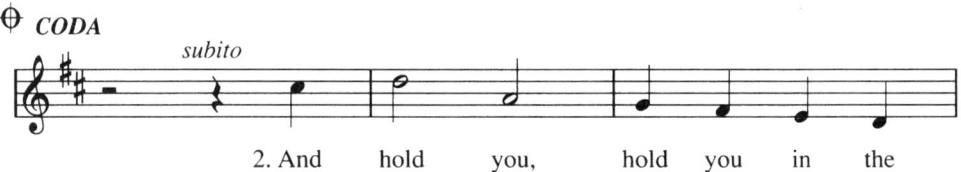

WORDS and MUSIC: Michael Joncas
© 1979, 1991, New Dawn Music, 5536 NE Hassalo, Portland, OR 97213.
All Rights Reserved. Used with Permission.

THE SERVICE OF THE WORD

113 Psalm 98: Sing a New Song to the Lord

1. Sing a new song to the Lord, he to whom wonders belong! Rejoice in his triumph and tell of his power— O sing to the Lord a new song!
2. Now to the ends of the earth see his salvation is shown! And still he remembers his mercy and truth, unchanging in love to his own.
3. Sing a new song and rejoice, publish his praises abroad! Let voices in chorus, with trumpet and horn, resound for the joy of the Lord!
4. Join with the hills and the sea thunders of praise to prolong! In judgment and justice he comes to the earth— O sing to the Lord a new song!

WORDS: Timothy Dudley-Smith, 1971; para. of Psalm 98
MUSIC: David G. Wilson, 1971
Copyright © 1973 by Hope Publishing Co., Carol Stream, IL 60188. All Rights Reserved.

ONSLOW SQUARE
7.7.11.8.

THE SERVICE OF THE WORD

2. The Lord is com-pas-sion and love, slow to

an-ger and rich in mer-cy. He does not treat us ac-cord-ing to our

sins nor re-pay us ac-cord-ing to our faults.

3. As a Fa-ther has com-pas-sion on his chil-dren, the Lord has

pi-ty on those who fear Him; for He knows of what we are

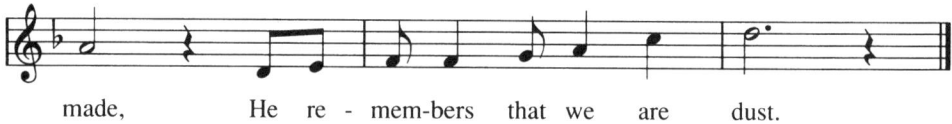
made, He re-mem-bers that we are dust.

116 Psalm 116: What Shall I Render to the Lord?

1. What shall I render to the Lord for all his benefits to me? How shall my life, by grace restored, give worthy thanks, O Lord, to Thee?
2. Salvation's cup of blessing now I take and call upon God's name. Before his saints I pay my vow and here my gratitude proclaim.
3. His saints the Lord delights to save; their death is precious in his sight. He has redeemed me from the grave, and in his service I delight.
4. With thankful heart I offer now my gift and call upon God's name. Before his saints I pay my vow and here my gratitude proclaim.
5. Within his house, the house of prayer, I dedicate myself to God. Let all his saints his grace declare and join to sound his praise abroad.

WORDS: Psalm 116:12–19; vers. Psalter, 1912
MUSIC: Second Supplement to Psalmody in Miniature, c. 1780; adapt. Edward Miller, 1790

ROCKINGHAM
LM

SONGS FROM THE PSALMS

Psalm 122: I Rejoiced When I Heard Them Say 117

WORDS and MUSIC: John Michael Talbot
© 1990 Birdwing Music/Cherry Lane Music Publishing Co., Inc.
Admin. by EMI Christian Music Publishing.
All Rights Reserved. Reprinted by Permission.

THE SERVICE OF THE WORD

120 Exodus 15:1,2: I Will Sing unto the Lord

*An optional stanza for use at Easter.

WORDS: From the Song of Moses and Miriam, Exodus 15:1–2
MUSIC: Israeli folk song.
Harmonization: Emily R. Brink, 1986. © 1987, CRC Publications, Grand Rapids, MI 49560.
All Rights Reserved. Used by Permission.

TZENA
PM

OLD TESTAMENT SONGS

Judges 5: ¡Canta, Débora, Canta! 121

¡Can - ta, Dé - bo - ra, can - ta! ¡Can - ta, Dé - bo - ra, can - ta!

Moth - er in Is - ra - el, lead - er of her ar - mies,
We lift up our voic - es, ev - ery - one to - geth - er,
Ma - dre de Is - ra - el, lí - der de e - jér - ci - tos,
To - dos los que can - tan, al - cen hoy sus vo - ces,

sing a hymn of vic - tory to our God.
sing - ing the tri - umphs of our God.
can - ta un him - no a tu Se - ñor.
can - ten un him - no de lo - or.

Refrain

For our God is good! God is good and has
Por - que bue - no es Dios, bue - no es Dios, él es -

cho - sen those who are hum - ble. For our God is good!
co - ge a los hu - mil - des. Por - que bue - no es Dios,

God is good and will strength - en the peo - ple with might!
bue - no es Dios. Él los for - ta - le - ce con su po - der.

"Canta" is the Spanish word for "sing".
WORDS and MUSIC: Luiza Cruz, 1973; English translation by Gertrude C. Suppe, 1987;   DEBORA
Spanish translation by Raquel Gutiérrez-Achon, 1987; based on Judges 5.
Words, music © 1975, 1987 The United Methodist Publishing House;
trans. © 1989 The United Methodist Publishing House.

THE SERVICE OF THE WORD

122 Isaiah 12:3–6: The First Song of Isaiah

Refrain (Repeated at end)

Sure-ly, it is God who saves me; I will trust in Him and not be a-

fraid. For the Lord is my strong-hold and my sure de-fense, and

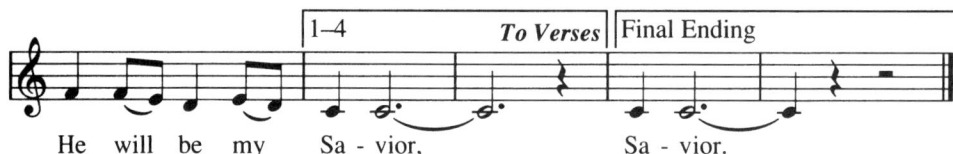
He will be my Sa - vior, Sa - vior.

Verses

1. There - fore you shall draw wa - ter with re - joic - ing

from the springs of sal - va - tion. And on that day you shall say, give

thanks to the Lord and call up - on his name;

2. Make his deeds known a-mong the peo - ples; see that they re-mem-ber that his

name is ex-alt - ed. Sing the prais-es of the Lord, for He has done great

WORDS: From *The Book of Common Prayer*
MUSIC: Jack Noble White
Copyright © 1977 by Charles Mortimer Guilbert as Custodian
Used by permission of The Church Hymnal Corporation
800 Second Avenue, New York, N.Y. 10017

OLD TESTAMENT SONGS

things, and this is known in all the world.

3. Cry a - loud in - hab - i - tants of Zi - on,

ring out your joy, for the great one in the

midst of you is the Ho - ly One of Is - rael.

Isaiah 60: Arise, Shine, for Your Light Is Come 123

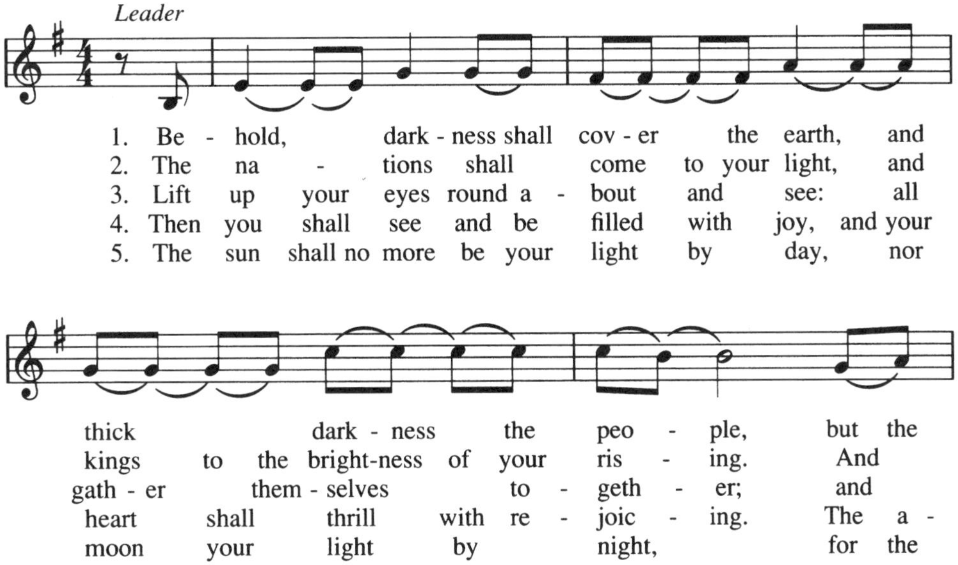

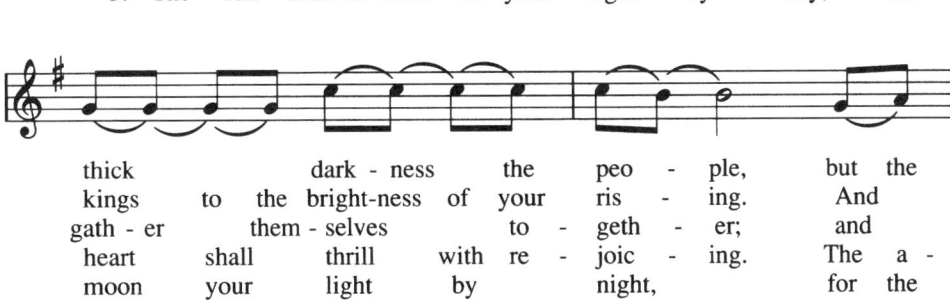

1. Be - hold, dark - ness shall cov - er the earth, and
2. The na - tions shall come to your light, and
3. Lift up your eyes round a - bout and see: all
4. Then you shall see and be filled with joy, and your
5. The sun shall no more be your light by day, nor

thick dark - ness the peo - ple, but the
kings to the bright-ness of your ris - ing. And
gath - er them - selves to - geth - er; and
heart shall thrill with re - joic - ing. The a -
moon your light by night, for the

WORDS: Isaiah 60:1–5, 14, 20: para. Eric Glass, 1974, alt.
MUSIC: Eric Glass, 1974; arr. Dale Grotenhuis, 1986
© 1974 by GORDON V. THOMPSON MUSIC. A Divsion of WARNER/CHAPPELL MUSIC CANADA LTD.
All Rights Reserved. Used by Permission.

ARISE, SHINE
Irregular

THE SERVICE OF THE WORD

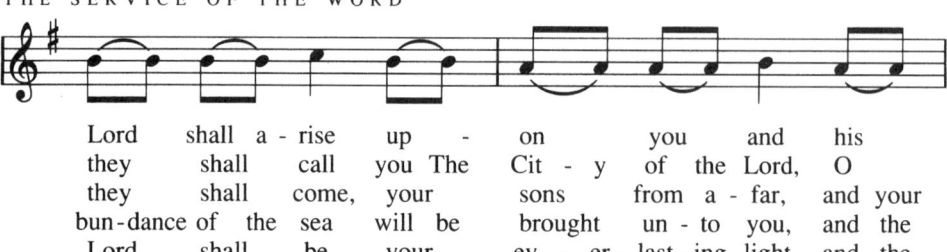

Lord   shall a - rise   up   -   on   you   and   his
they   shall   call   you The   Cit - y   of   the Lord,   O
they   shall   come,   your   sons   from a - far,   and   your
bun-dance of   the   sea   will   be   brought   un - to   you,   and   the
Lord   shall   be   your   ev - er - last - ing light,   and   the

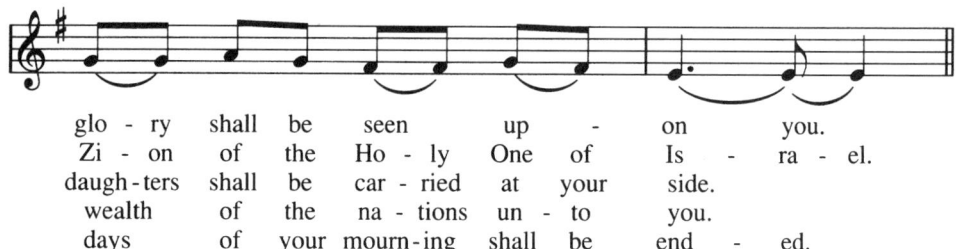

glo - ry   shall   be   seen   up   -   on   you.
Zi - on   of   the   Ho - ly   One   of   Is - ra - el.
daugh-ters   shall   be   car - ried   at   your   side.
wealth   of   the   na - tions   un - to   you.
days   of   your mourn-ing   shall   be   end   -   ed.

Congregation

A - rise,   shine,   for your   light   is   come, and   the   glo - ry of the

Lord   is   ris - en.   O, a - rise,   shine,   for your   light   is

come,   and   the   glo - ry   of   the   Lord   is   up   -   on   you.

OLD TESTAMENT SONGS

Joel 2, 3: Fear Not, Rejoice and Be Glad 124

Refrain
Fear not, re-joice and be glad: the Lord has done a great thing,

has poured out His Spir-it on all who live, on those who con-fess His name.

1. The fig tree is bud-ding, the vine bear-ing fruit, the
2. We shall eat in plen-ty and be sat-is-fied, the
3. "My peo-ple will know that I am the Lord; their

wheat fields are gold-en with grain. Thrust in the sick-le, the
moun-tains will drip with new wine. "My chil-dren will drink of the
shame I have tak-en a - way. My Spir-it will lead them to -

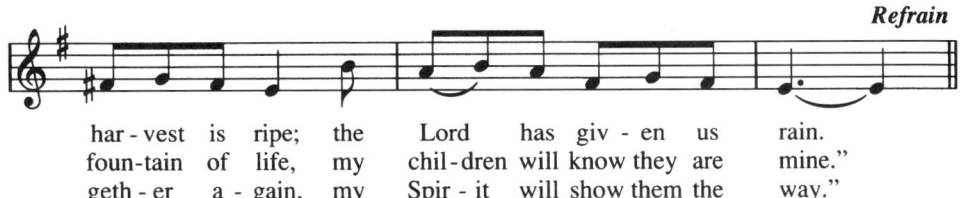
Refrain
har - vest is ripe; the Lord has giv - en us rain.
foun-tain of life, my chil-dren will know they are mine."
geth - er a - gain, my Spir - it will show them the way."

WORDS: based on Joel 2–3; vers. Priscilla Wright, 1971, alt.
MUSIC: Priscilla Wright, 1971; harm. Dale Grotenhuis, 1986
© 1971 CELEBRATION (Administered by THE COPYRIGHT COMPANY, Nashville, TN)
All Rights Reserved. International Copyright Secured. Used by Permission.

CLAY
Irregular

THE SERVICE OF THE WORD

125 Jonah's Song

1. In my trou-ble, in my trou-ble I cried out to the
2. I was sink-ing, I was sink-ing in dark-ness to the
3. Those who wor-ship worth-less i-dols will nev-er know the

Lord, my God, and,
o - cean floor, and, Lord, You heard me,
grace of God, but,

yes, You heard me, from the depths You heard my

cry.
Though the wa-ter swirled a-round me,
When my prayer came to your tem-ple,
With a song of high thanks-giv-ing

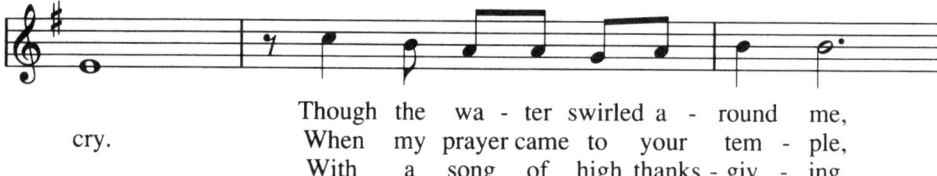

though the deep waves thun-dered o'er me,
You stretched out your might-y hand. Lord, You saved me,
I will sac-ri-fice to God.

yes, You saved me. You would not let your ser-vant die.

WORDS: Edith Bajema, 1993
MUSIC: Vicki Williams, 1994
© 1994, CRC Publications, Grand Rapids, MI 49650. All Rights Reserved. Used by Permission.

OLD TESTAMENT SONGS

Hosea: Come Back to Me 126

1. Come back to me with all your heart. Don't let fear
2. The wil-der-ness will lead you to your heart
3. You shall sleep se-cure with peace; faith-ful-ness

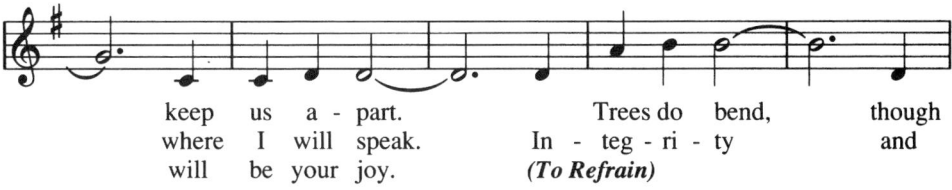

keep us a - part. Trees do bend, though
where I will speak. In - teg - ri - ty and
will be your joy. *(To Refrain)*

straight and tall; So must we to oth-ers' call.
jus - tice with ten-der-ness you shall know.

Refrain

Long have I wait-ed for your com - ing home to me and

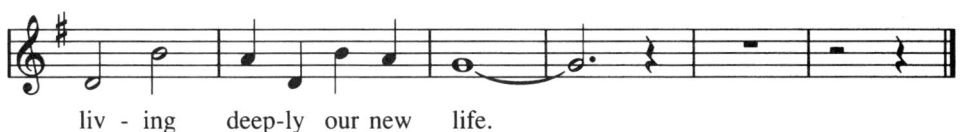

liv - ing deep-ly our new life.

WORDS: Hosea 6:1; 3:3; 2:16, 21
MUSIC: Gregory Norbet
Copyright © 1972 from the recording LISTEN, The Benedictine Foundation
of the State of Vermont, Inc. Weston, Vermont USA

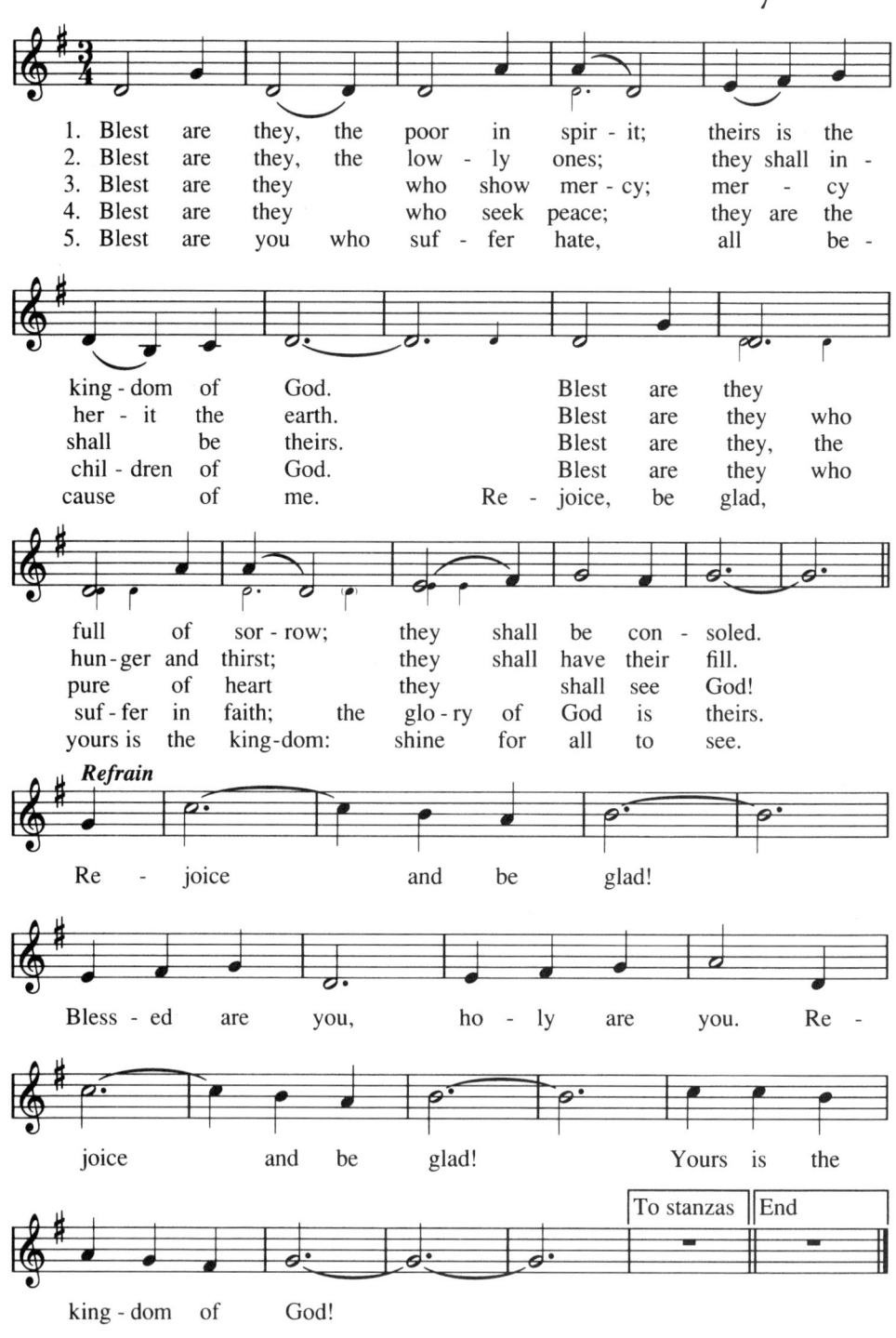

131 Luke 1:46–49: Magnify the Lord

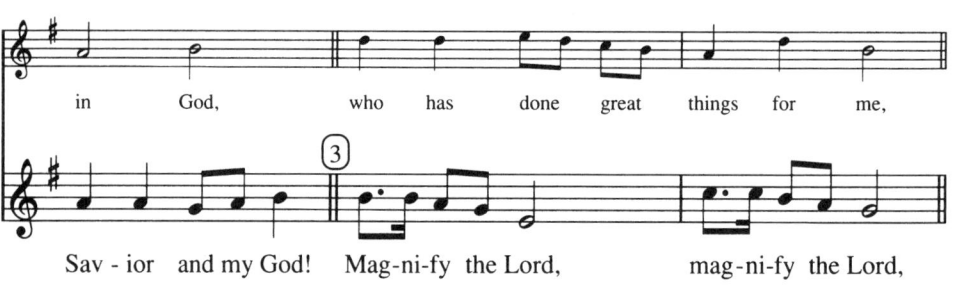

WORDS: from the Song of Mary, Luke 1:46-49; para. Bert Polman, 1985
MUSIC: Jacques Berthier, 1984
Copyright © 1984 by G.I.A. Publications, Inc., Chicago, Illinois.
All Rights Reserved. Used by Permission.

MAGNIFICAT
PM

THE SERVICE OF THE WORD

133 Phil. 2:6–11: At the Name of Jesus

1. At the name of Jesus every knee shall bow,
every tongue confess Him King of Glory now;
'tis the Father's pleasure we should call Him Lord,

2. Humbled for a season, to receive a name
from the lips of sinners unto whom He came;
faithfully He bore it spotless to the last,

3. Bore it up triumphant with its human light,
through all ranks of creatures to the central height;
to the eternal Godhead, to the Father's throne,

4. In your hearts enthrone Him; there let Him subdue
all that is not holy, all that is not true;
crown Him as your captain in temptations's hour,

5. Christians, this Lord Jesus shall return again,
with His Father's glory, with His angel train,
for all wreaths of empire meet upon His brow,

WORDS: Caroline M. Noel, 1870, alt.
MUSIC: Michael Brierley, 1960
Music © 1960 Josef Weinberger Limited.
Reproduced by permission of the copyright owners.

CAMBERWELL
6.5.6.5.D.

NEW TESTAMENT SONGS

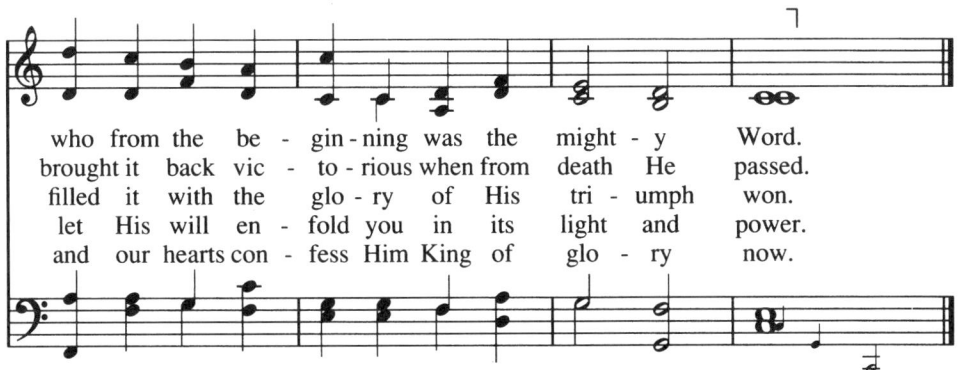

who from the be - gin - ning was the might - y Word.
brought it back vic - to - rious when from death He passed.
filled it with the glo - ry of His tri - umph won.
let His will en - fold you in its light and power.
and our hearts con - fess Him King of glo - ry now.

Phil. 1:6: He Who Began a Good Work 134

Chorus
♩ = 100

He who be - gan a good work in you,

He who be - gan a good work in you

will be faith - ful to com-plete it,

He'll be faith - ful to com-plete it, He who start-

2nd time to Coda

- ed the work will be faith - ful to com-plete it in you.

WORDS and MUSIC: Jon Mohr
© Copyright 1987, 1995 Jonathan Mark Music/ASCAP (Admin. by Gaither Copyright Management)
and Birdwing Music/ASCAP (admin. by EMI Christian Music Publishing).
All Rights Reserved. Used by Permission.

THE SERVICE OF THE WORD

NEW TESTAMENT SONGS

Rev. 5:12: Glory to the Lamb 135

Glo - ry, glo - ry, glo - ry to the Lamb.

Glo - ry, glo - ry, glo - ry to the Lamb. For he is

glo - ri - ous and wor - thy to be praised, the

Lamb up - on the throne; and un - to him we

lift our voice in praise, the Lamb up - on the throne.

WORDS and MUSIC: Larry Dempsey
© 1983 ZionSong Music, P.O. Box 574044, Orlando, FL 32857.
All Rights Reserved. International Copyright Secured. Used by Permission.

Alleluia Songs

136 Alleluia

1. Al-le-lu-ia, Al-le-lu-ia, Al-le-lu-ia, Al-le-lu-ia, Al-le-lu-ia, Al-le-lu-ia, Al-le-lu-ia, Al-le-lu-ia!
2. He's my Sav-ior, Al-le-lu-ia, he's my Sav-ior, Al-le-lu-ia, he's my Sav-ior, Al-le-lu-ia, he's my Sav-ior, Al-le-lu-ia!
3. He is wor-thy, Al-le-lu-ia, he is wor-thy, Al-le-lu-ia, he is wor-thy, Al-le-lu-ia, he is wor-thy, Al-le-lu-ia!
4. I will praise him, Al-le-lu-ia, I will praise him, Al-le-lu-ia, I will praise him, Al-le-lu-ia, I will praise him, Al-le-lu-ia!
5. *Mar-a-nath-a, Al-le-lu-ia, Mar-a-nath-a, Al-le-lu-ia, Mar-a-nath-a, Al-le-lu-ia, Mar-a-nath-a, Al-le-lu-ia!

*O Lord, come.

WORDS and MUSIC: Jerry Sinclair, 1972
© Copyright 1972 by MANNA MUSIC, INC., 35255 Brooten Road, Pacific City, OR 97135.
All Rights Reserved. Used by Permission.

ALLELUIA
L.M.

ALLELUIA SONGS

Heleluyan (Alleluia) 137

Pronounced: Hay-lay-loo-yahn.

WORDS and MUSIC: Traditional Muscogee (Creek) Indian;
Transcription by Charles H. Webb
Transcription © 1989 The United Methodist Publishing House.

HELELUYAN

Alleluia 138

MUSIC: Jacques Berthier, 1982.
Music copyright © 1982, 1983, 1984 by Les Presses de Taizé (France).
Used by permission of G.I.A. Publications, Inc., Chicago, Illinois exclusive agent All Rights Reserved.

TAIZÉ ALLELUIA

THE SERVICE OF THE WORD

139 Halle, Halle, Hallelujah

MUSIC: Caribbean traditional; arr. Mark Sedio, b. 1954
Arrangement is reprinted by permission from WITH ONE VOICE,
copyright © 1995 Augsburg Fortress.

Invitational Songs

❖ ❖ ❖

Just As I Am, Without One Plea 140

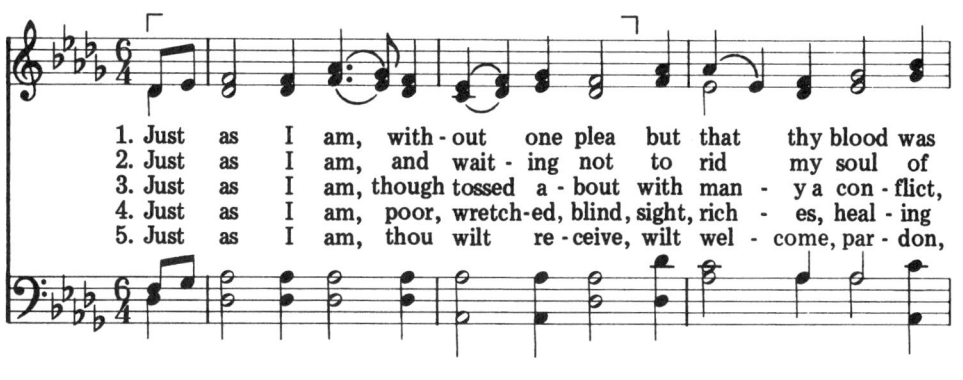

1. Just as I am, with-out one plea but that thy blood was
2. Just as I am, and wait-ing not to rid my soul of
3. Just as I am, though tossed a-bout with man-y a con-flict,
4. Just as I am, poor, wretch-ed, blind, sight, rich-es, heal-ing
5. Just as I am, thou wilt re-ceive, wilt wel-come, par-don,

shed for me, and that thou bidd'st me come to thee, O
one dark blot, to thee whose blood can cleanse each spot, O
man-y a doubt, fight-ings and fears with-in, with-out, O
of the mind, yea, all I need in thee I find, O
cleanse, re-lieve; be-cause thy prom-ise I be-lieve, O

Coda (after Verse 5)

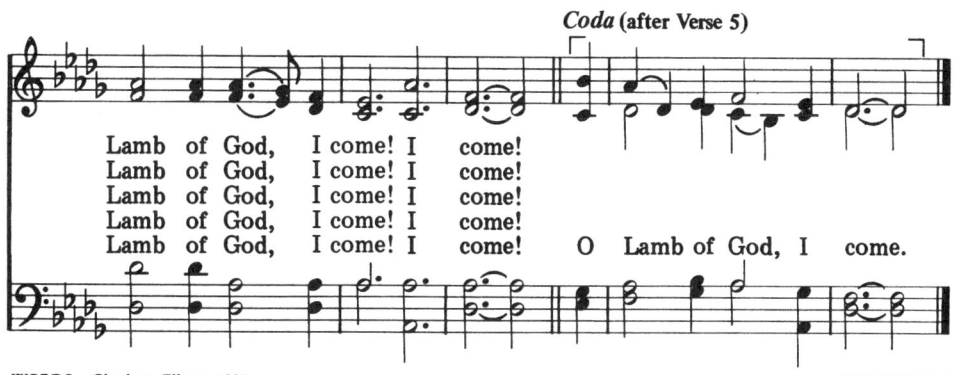

Lamb of God, I come! I come!
Lamb of God, I come! I come!
Lamb of God, I come! I come!
Lamb of God, I come! I come!
Lamb of God, I come! I come! O Lamb of God, I come.

WORDS: Charlotte Elliott, 1834
MUSIC: William B. Bradbury, 1849

WOODWORTH
L.M.Coda

INVITATIONAL SONGS

Obey My Voice 142

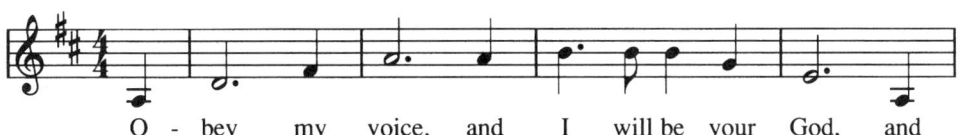
O - bey my voice, and I will be your God, and

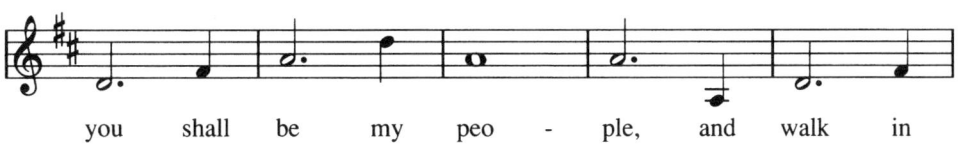
you shall be my peo - ple, and walk in

all the ways I have com - mand - ed you, that it may be

well with you and I will be your God. O - bey my

voice, and I will be your God, and you shall

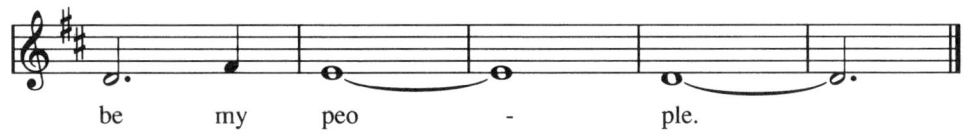
be my peo - ple.

WORDS: based on Jeremiah 7:23, KJV
MUSIC: Sheilagh Nowacki, 1970, *Festival of the Holy Spirit Song Book*, 1972
Music © by Sheilagh Nowacki, Beech Grove, IN 46107.
All Rights Reserved. Used by Permission.

THE SERVICE OF THE WORD

143 Change My Heart, O God

Change my heart, O God, make it ev-er true;

Change my heart, O God, may I be like You.

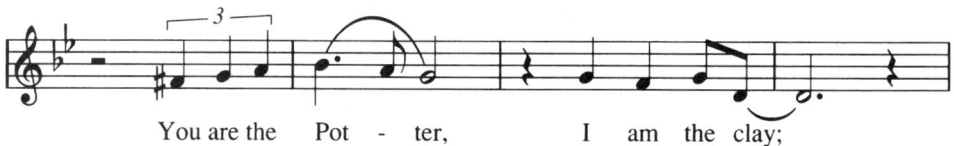
You are the Pot - ter, I am the clay;

Mold me and make me, this is what I pray.

Change my heart, O God, make it ev-er true;

Change my heart, O God, may I be like You.

WORDS and MUSIC: Eddie Espinosa
© 1982 by Mercy Publishing.

THE SERVICE OF THE WORD

145 Lord, I Want to Be a Christian

WORDS and MUSIC: African-American Spiritual

I WANT TO BE A CHRISTIAN
Irregular

INVITATIONAL SONGS

O Lord, Your Tenderness 146

O Lord, your ten-der-ness, melt-ing all my

bit-ter-ness; O Lord, I re-ceive your love.

O Lord, your love-li-ness, chang-ing my un-

worth-i-ness; O Lord, I re-ceive your Love.

O Lord, I re-ceive your Love;

O Lord, I re-ceive your love.

WORDS and MUSIC: Graham Kendrick
© 1986 Kingsway's Thankyou Music/Adm. in N., S. & C. America by Integrity's Hosanna! Music.
c/o Integrity Music, Inc., P.O. Box 851622, Mobile, AL 36685.
All Rights Reserved. International Copyright Secured. Used by Permission.

Dedication Songs

The Servant Song 148

1. Broth - er, let me be your ser - vant, let me be as
2. We are pil - grims on a jour - ney, we are broth - ers
3. I will hold the Christ-light for you, in the night - time
4. I will weep when you are weep - ing, when you laugh I'll
5. When we sing to God in heav - en, we shall find such
6. Sis - ter, let me be your ser - vant, let me be as

Christ to you. Pray that I might have the grace to
on the road, we are here to help each oth - er
of your fear, I will hold my hand out to you,
laugh with you, I will share your joy and sor - row
har - mo - ny, born of all we've known to - ge - ther
Christ to you. Pray that I might have the grace to

let you be my ser - vant, too.
walk the mile and bear the load.
speak the peace you long to hear.
till we've seen this jour - ney through.
of Christ's love and ag - on - y.
let you be my ser - vant, too.

WORDS and MUSIC: Richard Gillard
© 1977 SCRIPTURES IN SONG, DIV. INTEGRITY MUSIC (Administered by THE COPYRIGHT COMPANY, Nashville, TN) All Rights Reserved. International Copyright Secured. Used by Permission.

DEDICATION SONGS

THE SERVICE OF THE WORD

150 Take My Life That It May Be

1. Take my life that it may be all You purpose, Lord, for me. Take my moments and my days; let them sing your endless praise.
2. Take my hands and let them move at the impulse of your love. Take my feet and lead their way; never let them go astray.
3. Take my voice and let me sing always, only, for my King. Take my lips and keep them true, filled with messages from You.
4. Take my wealth, all I possess; make me rich in faithfulness. Take my mind that I may use every power as You shall choose.

5. Take my motives and my will,
all your purpose to fulfill.
Take my heart—it is your own;
it shall be your royal throne.

6. Take my love; my Lord, I pour
at your feet its treasure store.
Take myself, and I will be
yours for all eternity.

WORDS: Frances R. Havergal, 1874; revised *Psalter Hymnal*, 1987
MUSIC: Timothy Hoekman, 1979
© 1987, CRC Publications, Grand Rapids, MI 49560.
All Rights Reserved. Used by Permission.

TEBBEN
77 77

DEDICATION SONGS

Bring Forth the Kingdom 153

Verses
Leader

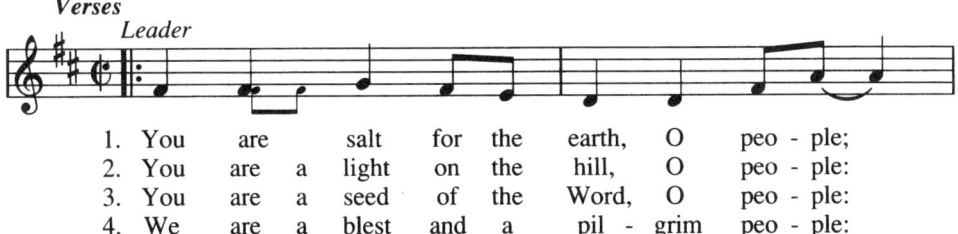

1. You are salt for the earth, O people;
2. You are a light on the hill, O people:
3. You are a seed of the Word, O people;
4. We are a blest and a pilgrim people:

All   *Leader*

salt for the kingdom of God! Share the flavor of
light for the city of God! Shine so holy and
bring forth the kingdom of God! Seeds of mercy and
bound for the kingdom of God! Love our journey and

All

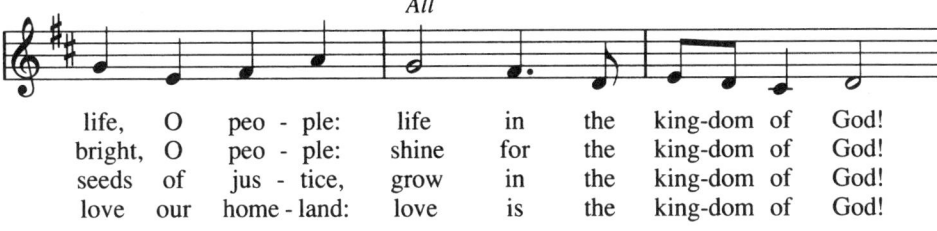

life, O people: life in the kingdom of God!
bright, O people: shine for the kingdom of God!
seeds of justice, grow in the kingdom of God!
love our homeland: love is the kingdom of God!

Refrain

Bring forth the kingdom of mercy, bring forth the

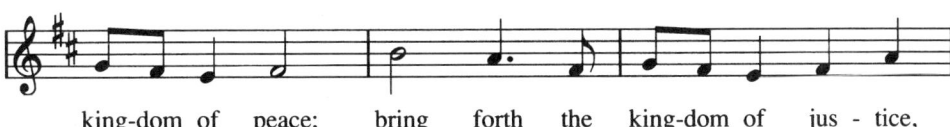

kingdom of peace; bring forth the kingdom of justice,

bring forth the city of God!

WORDS: Matthew 5:13-15; Marty Haugen, b. 1950
MUSIC: Marty Haugen, b. 1950
Copyright © 1986 by G.I.A. Publications, Inc., Chicago, Illinois.
All Rights Reserved. Used by Permission.

THE SERVICE OF THE WORD

154 Sent by the Lord

Sent by the Lord am I; my hands are read-y now to

make the earth the place in which the king-dom comes.

The an-gels can-not change a world of hurt and pain in-

to a world of love, of jus-tice and of peace. The

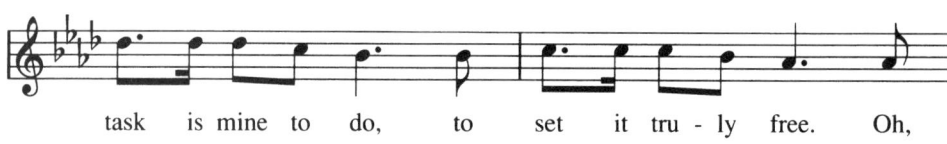
task is mine to do, to set it tru-ly free. Oh,

help me to o-bey; help me to do your will.

WORDS: Cuban oral tradition; translated by Jorge Maldonado, 1991
MUSIC: Traditional Cuban; arranged by Iona Community, 1991
Music arr. © 1991 by The Iona (Scotland) Community.
Used by Permission of G.I.A. Publications, Inc., Chicago, Illinois, exclusive agent. All Rights Reserved.

DEDICATION SONGS

The Gift of Love 155

1. Though I may speak with brav-est fire, and have the
2. Though I may give all I pos-sess, and striv-ing
3. Come, Spir-it, come, our hearts con-trol, our spir-its

gift to all in - spire, and have not love:
so my love pro - fess, but not be given
long to be made whole. Let in - ward love

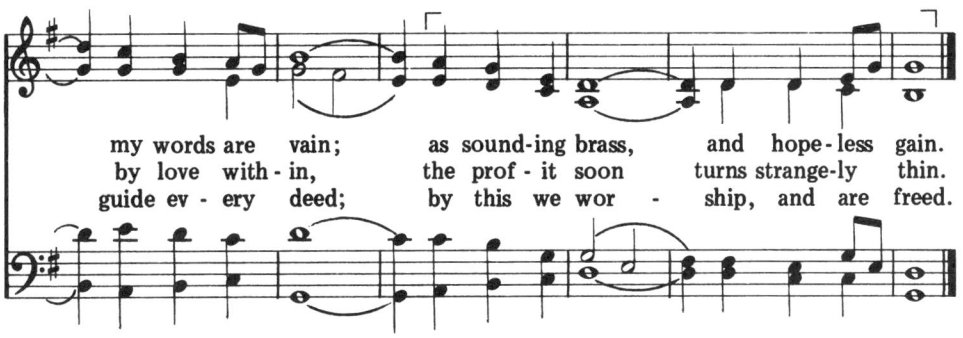

my words are vain; as sound-ing brass, and hope-less gain.
by love with - in, the prof - it soon turns strange-ly thin.
guide ev - ery deed; by this we wor - ship, and are freed.

WORDS: Hal Hopson, 1972; para. of 1 Corinthians 13
MUSIC: Hal Hopson, 1971; based on Traditional English melody
Copyright © 1972 Hope Publishing Co., Carol Stream, IL 60188. All Rights Reserved.

GIFT OF LOVE
L.M.

Creedal Songs

156 We Believe (in God the Father)

1. We believe in God the Father, maker of the universe.
And in Christ the Son, our Savior, come to us by virgin birth.
We believe He died to save us, bore our sins, was crucified;
then, from death, He rose victorious ascended to the Father's side.

2. We believe He sends His Spirit on His church with gifts of pow'r.
God, His Word of truth affirming, sends us to the nations now.
He will come again in glory judge the living and the dead;
ev'ry knee shall bow before Him, then must ev'ry tongue confess.

Refrain
Jesus, Lord of all, Lord of all;
Jesus, Lord of all, Lord of all.
Jesus, Lord of all, Lord of all;
Jesus, Lord of all, Lord of all.

WORDS and MUSIC: Graham Kendrick
© 1986 by Make Way Music/Adm. in N., S. & C. America by Integrity's Hosanna! Music.
c/o Integrity Music, Inc., P.O. Box 851622, Mobile, AL 36685.
All Rights Reserved. International Copyright Secured. Used by Permission.

What a Mighty God 159

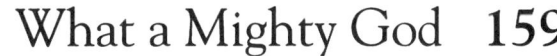

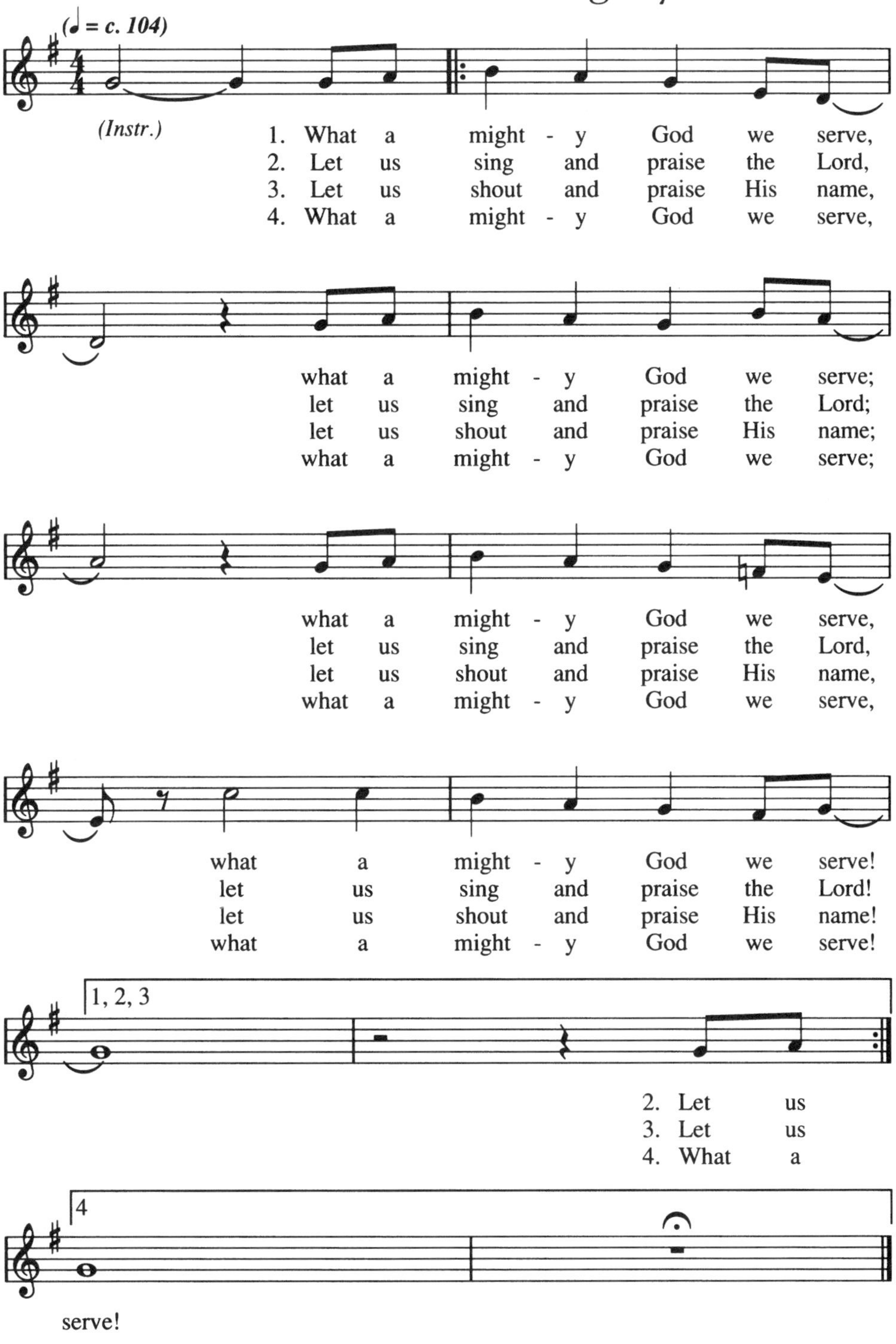

WORDS and MUSIC: African Folk Song, Adapted by Jack Schrader

CREEDAL SONGS

Every Eye Shall See 162

WORDS: William J. Gaither and Gloira Gaither, 1980
MUSIC: William J. Gaither, 1980
© Copyright 1980, 1995 William J. Gaither. All Rights Reserved. Used by Permission.

EVERY EYE
Irregular

163 All Heaven Declares

Majestically

1. All heav'n de-clares   the glo-ry of the ris-en Lord.
2. I will pro-claim   the glo-ry of the ris-en Lord,

Who can com-pare   with the beau-ty of the Lord?
who once was slain   to rec-on-cile us to God.

For-ev-er He will be   the Lamb up-on the throne;
For-ev-er He will be   the Lamb up-on the throne;

last time only

I glad-ly bow the knee   and wor-ship Him a-lone.
I glad-ly bow the knee   and wor-ship Him a-lone.

WORDS and MUSIC: Noel and Tricia Richards
Copyright © 1987 Thankyou Music. Admin. by MARANATHA! MUSIC
All Rights Reserved. International Copyright Secured.

164 Christ Beside Me

Unison

1. Christ be-side me, Christ be-fore me,
2. Christ on my right hand, Christ on my left hand,
3. Christ be in all hearts think-ing a-bout me,
4. Christ be-side me, Christ be-fore me,

WORDS: Adapt. James Quinn, alt., from *St. Patrick's Breastplate*.
MUSIC: Trad. Gaelic melody, Arr. Jack Schrader.
Music used by permission of Oxford University Press fro the *Revised Church Hymnary 1927*.

BUNESSAN
5.5.5.4.D.

CREEDAL SONGS

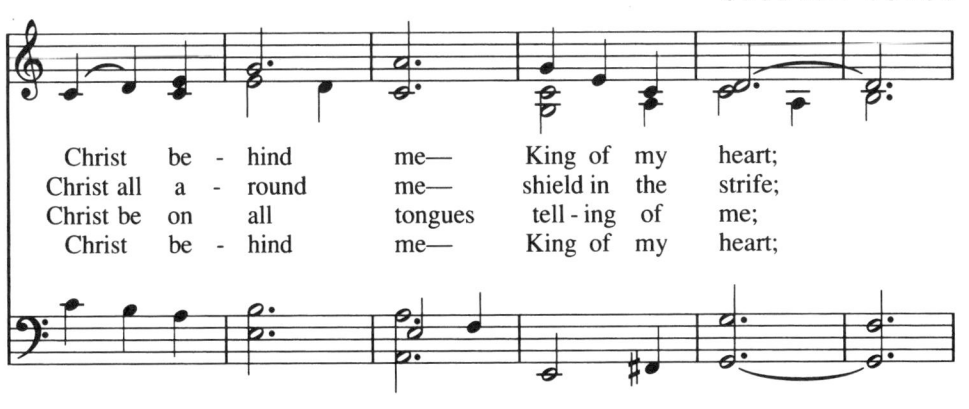

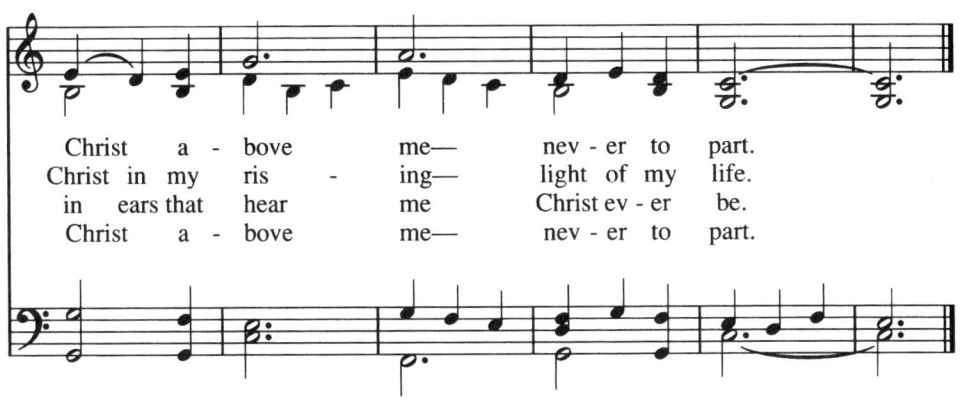

165 I Bind unto Myself Today

I bind unto myself today the strong name of the Trinity,
    by invocation of the same, the Three in One, and One in Three.

I bind this day to me forever by power of faith Christ's incarnation,
    his baptism in the Jordan river, his death on the cross for my salvation;
his bursting from the spiced tomb, his riding up the heavenly way,
    his coming at the day of doom I bind unto myself today.

I bind unto myself today the power of God to hold and lead,
    his eye to watch, his might to stay, his ear to harken to my need,
the wisdom of my God to teach, his hand to guide, his shield to ward,
    the Word of God to give me speech, his heavenly host to be my guard.

> *Christ be with me, Christ within me,*
>   *Christ behind me, Christ before me,*
> *Christ beside me, Christ to win me;*
>   *Christ to comfort and restore me;*
> *Christ beneath me, Christ above me,*
>   *Christ in quiet, Christ in danger,*
> *Christ in hearts of all that love me,*
>   *Christ in mouth of friend and stranger.*

I bind unto myself the name, the strong name of the Trinity,
    by invocation of the same, the Three in One, and One in Three,
of whom all nature hath creation, eternal Father, Spirit, Word;
    praise to the God of my salvation, salvation is of Christ the Lord!

St. Patrick, c. 430; paraphrased, Cecil Frances Alexander, 1889
Tradition ascribes the original of this hymn to St. Patrick (372–466)
who gave much of his life to missionary work in Ireland. It was believed that this
affirmation would protect a Christian from "demons, human enemies, and vices."

CREEDAL SONGS

Fairest Lord Jesus 166

WORDS: *Gesangbuch*, Münster, 1677; tr. anonymous, 1850; st. 2, tr. Joseph A. Seiss, 1873
MUSIC: H. A. Hoffman von Fallersleben's *Schlesische Volkslieder*, 1842; arr. Richard S. Willis, 1850

CRUSADER'S HYMN
5.6.8.5.5.8.

PRAYER SONGS

If You Believe and I Believe 168

If you believe and I believe and we together pray,
the Holy Spirit will come down and set God's people free,
and set God's people free, and set God's people free;
the Holy Spirit will come down and set God's people free.

WORDS: from Zimbabwe, based on Matthew 18:19
MUSIC: from Zimbabwe, as adapted from an English song

THE SERVICE OF THE WORD

169 Stay with Me

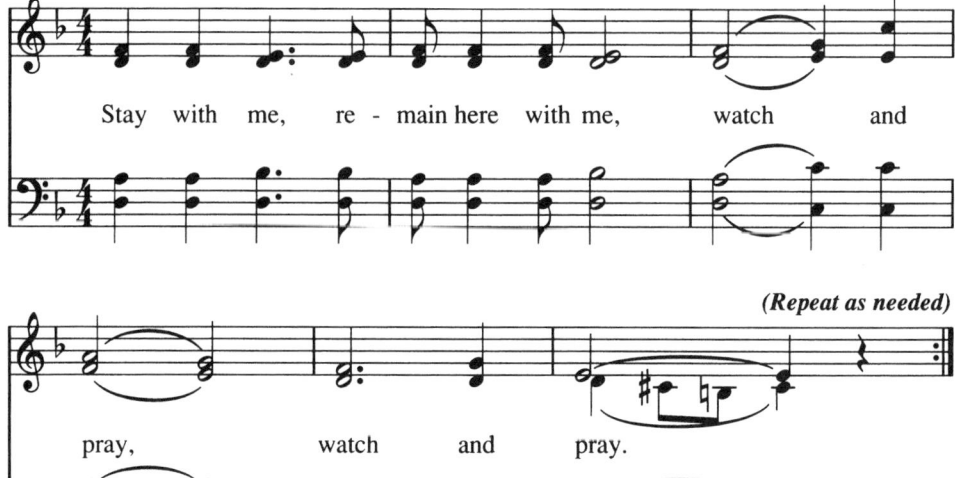

WORDS: Based on Matthew 26
MUSIC: Jacques Berthier
Music copyright © 1982 Les Presses de Taizé (France). Used by permission of G.I.A. Publications, Inc.,
Chicago, Illinois, exclusive agent. All Rights Reserved.

170 Stay Here

WORDS: Based on Matt. 26
MUSIC: From the Taizé community
Copyright © 1982 by Les Presses de Taizé (France). Used by permission of G.I.A. Publications, Inc.,
Chicago, Illinois, exclusive agent. All Rights Reserved.

PRAYER SONGS

Let Us Pray to the Lord 171

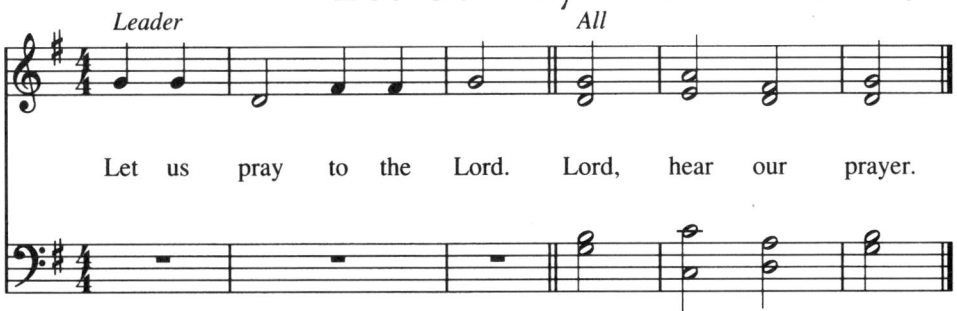

Let us pray to the Lord. Lord, hear our prayer.

WORDS: Traditional Prayer Response
MUSIC: Byzantine Chant

Lord, Be Glorified 172

1. In our lives, Lord, be glo-ri-fied, be glo-ri-fied,
2. In our homes, Lord, be glo-ri-fied, be glo-ri-fied,
3. In your church, Lord, be glo-ri-fied, be glo-ri-fied,
4. In your world, Lord, be glo-ri-fied, be glo-ri-fied,

in our lives, Lord, be glo-ri-fied to-day.
in our homes, Lord, be glo-ri-fied to-day.
in your church, Lord, be glo-ri-fied to-day.
in your world, Lord, be glo-ri-fied to-day.

WORDS and MUSIC: Bob Kilpatrick
EDITED: John Witvliet
© 1978 Bob Kilpatrick Music, P.O. Box 2383, Fair Oaks, CA 95628.
All Rights Reserved. Used by Permission

THE SERVICE OF THE WORD

173 O Lord Hear My Prayer

WORDS: Based on Psalm 102:1, 2
MUSIC: From the Taizé community
Copyright © 1982 Les Presses de Taizé (France). Used by permission of G.I.A. Publications, Inc.,
Chicago, Illinois, exclusive agent. All Rights Reserved.

THE SERVICE OF THE WORD

175 Lead Me, Lord

WORDS: Psalms 5:8, 4:8
MUSIC: Samuel Sebastian Wesley, 1861

LEAD ME, LORD
Irregular

THE SERVICE OF THE WORD

177 The Lord's Prayer

WORDS: Matthew 6:9–13, KJV
MUSIC: Albert Hay Malotte, 1935; arr. Donald P. Hustad, 1984
Copyright © 1935 (Renewed) by G. Schirmer, Inc. (ASCAP).
International Copyright Secured. All Rights Reserved. Reprinted by Permission.

MALOTTE
Irregular

THE SERVICE OF THE WORD

178 Our Father Who Art in Heaven

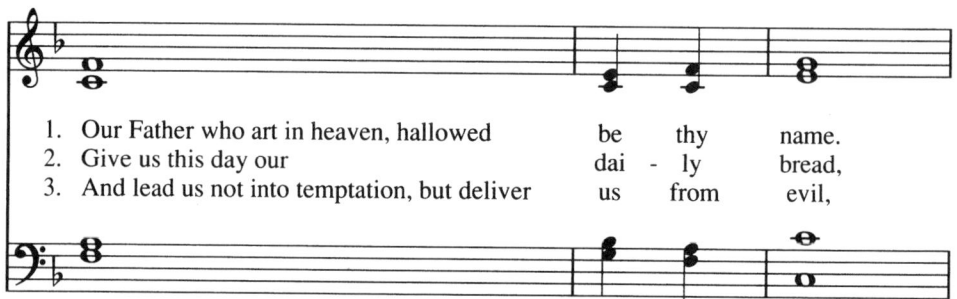

1. Our Father who art in heaven, hallowed be thy name.
2. Give us this day our dai - ly bread,
3. And lead us not into temptation, but deliver us from evil,

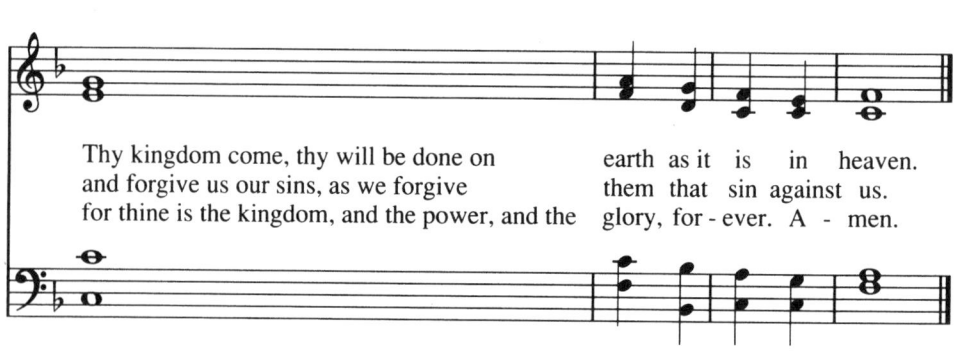

Thy kingdom come, thy will be done on earth as it is in heaven.
and forgive us our sins, as we forgive them that sin against us.
for thine is the kingdom, and the power, and the glory, for - ever. A - men.

WORDS: Matthew 6:8–13
MUSIC: Anonymous

PRAYER SONGS

Our Father 179
Pater noster

WORDS: *International Consultation on English Texts*
MUSIC: Betty Pulkingham
Music copyright © 1973 by G.I.A. Publications, Inc., Chicago, Illinois.
All Rights Reserved. Used by Permission.

THE SERVICE OF THE WORD

180 The Lord's Prayer (West Indian)

WORDS: Matthew 6:9–13; Adapt. by J. Jefferson Cleveland and Verolga Nix.
MUSIC: West Indian Folk Tune; Arr. by Carlton R. Young.
Adapt. © 1981 Abingdon Press; arr. © The United Methodist Publishing House.

WEST INDIAN
Irregular

Songs of Confession

✜ ✜ ✜

Create in Me a Clean Heart 181

Create in me a clean heart. O God, and renew a right spirit within me. Cre- Cast me not away from Your presence, O Lord, and take not Your Holy Spirit from me. Restore unto me the joy of Your salvation, and renew a right spirit within me.

WORDS: Based on Psalm 51:10-12
MUSIC: Unknown
© 1988 MARANATHA! MUSIC (Administered by THE COPYRIGHT COMPANY, Nashville, TN)
All Rights Reserved. International Copyright Secured. Used by Permission.

THE SERVICE OF THE WORD

182 Create in Me a Clean Heart

1. Create in me a clean heart, O God, and renew a right spirit within me.
2. Cast me not away from your presence, and take not your Holy Spirit from me.
3. Restore unto me the joy of your salvation, and uphold me with your free Spirit.

WORDS: Based on Psalm 51:10-12
MUSIC: *The Common Service Book and Hymnal,* 1917

SONGS OF CONFESSION

Sanctuary 185

WORDS and MUSIC: John Thompson and Randy Scruggs
© 1982 Whole Armor/Full Armor Administered by LITA Music/Justin Peters
3609 Donna Kay Drive, Nashville, TN 37211
All Rights Reserved. International Copyright Secured. Used by Permission.

THE SERVICE OF THE WORD

186 If My People

WORDS: Based on II Chron. 7:14
MUSIC: Eddie Smith
© 1992 MARANATHA! MUSIC (Administered by THE COPYRIGHT COMPANY, Nashville, TN)
All Rights Reserved. International Copyright Secured. Used by Permission.

THE SERVICE OF THE WORD

187 Purify My Heart

WORDS and MUSIC: Jeff Nelson
© 1993 Heartservice Music (admin. by Music Services)/MARANATHA! MUSIC
(Administered by THE COPYRIGHT COMPANY, Nashville, TN)
All Rights Reserved. International Copyright Secured. Used by Permission.

SONGS OF CONFESSION

Humble Thyself in the Sight of the Lord 188

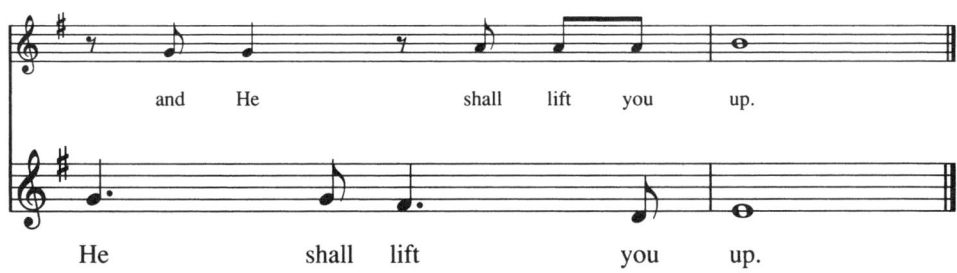

WORDS: James 4:10
MUSIC: Bob Hudson
© 1978 MARANATHA! MUSIC (Administered by THE COPYRIGHT COMPANY, Nashville, TN)
All Rights Reserved. International Copyright Secured. Used by Permission.

Songs of Assurance

❖ ❖ ❖

189 Amazing Grace! How Sweet the Sound

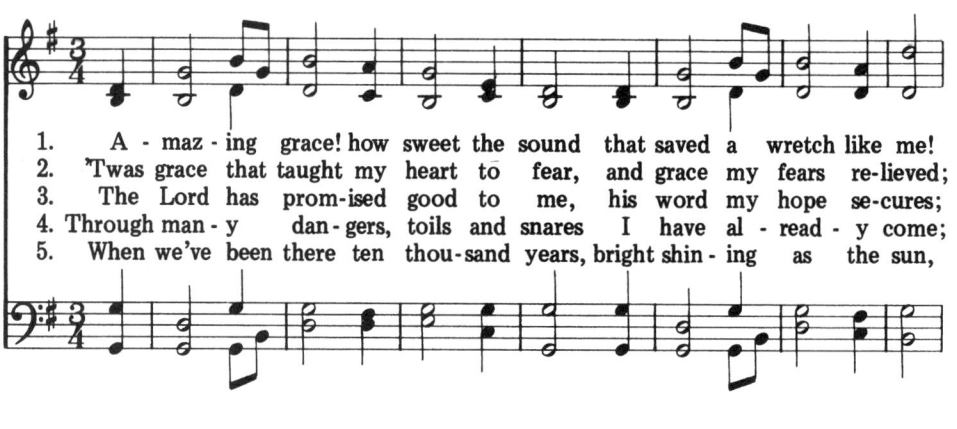

1. A-maz-ing grace! how sweet the sound that saved a wretch like me!
2. 'Twas grace that taught my heart to fear, and grace my fears re-lieved;
3. The Lord has prom-ised good to me, his word my hope se-cures.
4. Through man-y dan-gers, toils and snares I have al-read-y come;
5. When we've been there ten thou-sand years, bright shin-ing as the sun,

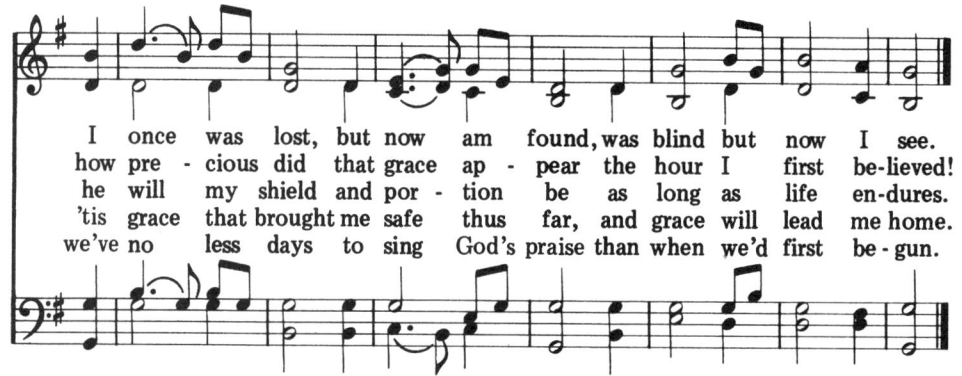

I once was lost, but now am found, was blind but now I see.
how pre-cious did that grace ap-pear the hour I first be-lieved!
he will my shield and por-tion be as long as life en-dures.
'tis grace that brought me safe thus far, and grace will lead me home.
we've no less days to sing God's praise than when we'd first be-gun.

WORDS: John Newton, 1779, alt.; st. 5, anonymous
MUSIC: *Virginia Harmony*, 1831; adapt. Edwin O. Excell, 1900

NEW BRITAIN
C.M.

SONGS OF ASSURANCE

Come, Let Us Reason 190

"Come, let us rea-son to-geth-er," that's what God says.

"Come, let us rea-son to-geth-er," says the Lord.

"Though your sins be as scar-let, they shall be as white as snow;

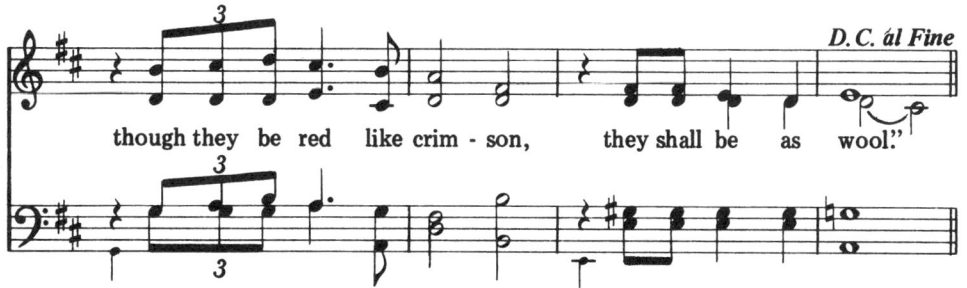
though they be red like crim-son, they shall be as wool."

WORDS: Ken Medema, 1971, from Isaiah 1:18
MUSIC: Ken Medema, 1971; arr. David Allen, 1986
© 1972 by Word Music (a div. of WORD, INC.) All Rights Reserved. Used by Permission.

COME LET US REASON
Irregular

THE SERVICE OF THE WORD

191 O Christ, the Healer, We Have Come

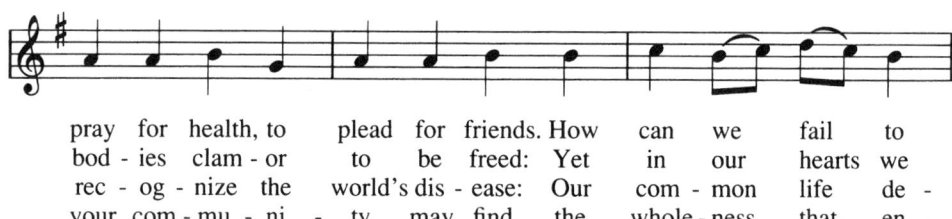

1. O Christ, the heal-er, we have come to
pray for health, to plead for friends. How can we fail to
be re - stored when reached by love that nev - er ends?

2. From ev - 'ry ail - ment flesh en - dures, our
bod - ies clam - or to be freed: Yet in our hearts we
would con - fess that whole-ness is our deep - est need.

3. In con - flicts that de - stroy our health we
rec - og - nize the world's dis - ease: Our com - mon life de -
clares our ills. Is there no cure, O Christ, for these?

4. Grant that we all, made one in faith, in
your com - mu - ni - ty may find the whole - ness that, en -
rich - ing us, shall reach and pros - per hu - man - kind.

WORDS: Fred Pratt Green   ERHALT UNS, HERR
MUSIC: *Geistliche Lieder*, 1543, Joseph Klug, c. 1500–c. 1552   LM
Words © 1969 by Hope Publishing Co., Carol Stream, IL 60188. All Rights Reserved.

192 Freely, Freely

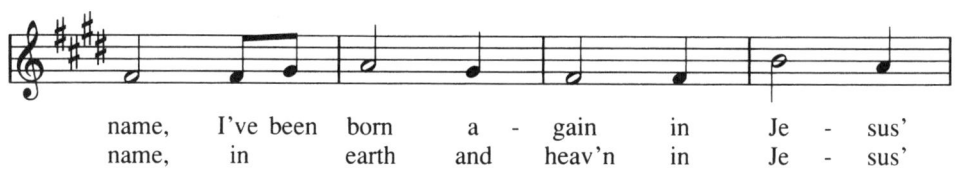

1. God for - gave my sin in Je - sus'
name, I've been born a - gain in Je - sus'

(2.) pow'r is giv'n in Je - sus'
name, in earth and heav'n in Je - sus'

WORDS: Based on Matt. 10:8b
MUSIC: Carol Owens
© 1972 Bud John Songs, Inc. Admin. by EMI Christian Music Publishing.
All Rights Reserved. Used by Permission.

SONGS OF ASSURANCE

name. And in Je - sus' name I come to
name. And in Je - sus' name I come to

you to share His love as He told me
you to share His pow'r as He told me

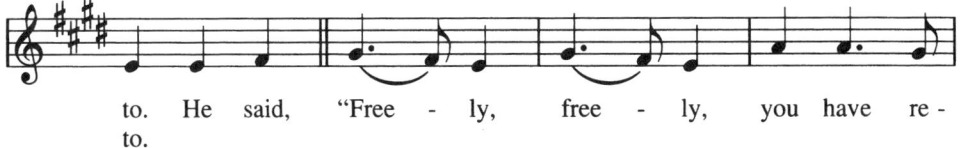
to. He said, "Free - ly, free - ly, you have re-
to.

ceived, free - ly, free - ly give.

Go in my name, and be - cause you be - lieve,

oth - ers will know that I live."   2. All

THE SERVICE OF THE WORD

194 Our Great Savior

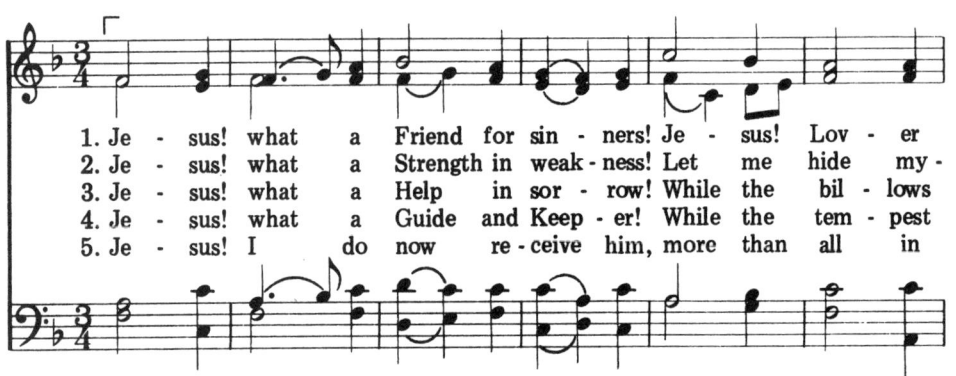

1. Je-sus! what a Friend for sin-ners! Je-sus! Lov-er
2. Je-sus! what a Strength in weak-ness! Let me hide my-
3. Je-sus! what a Help in sor-row! While the bil-lows
4. Je-sus! what a Guide and Keep-er! While the tem-pest
5. Je-sus! I do now re-ceive him, more than all in

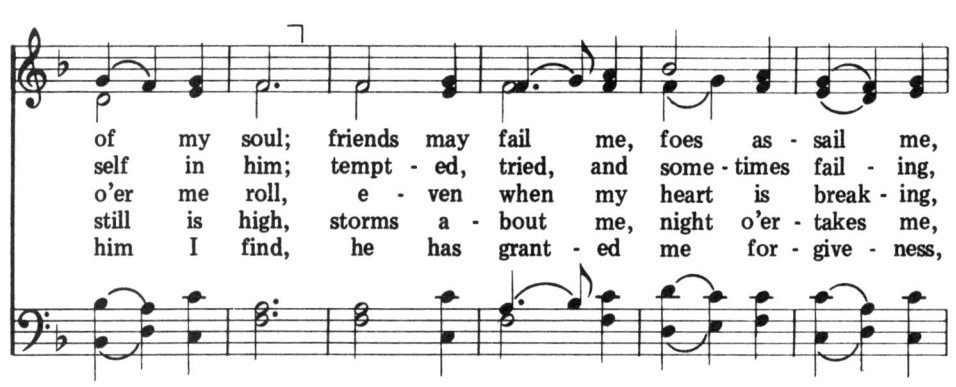

of my soul; friends may fail me, foes as-sail me,
self in him; tempt-ed, tried, and some-times fail-ing,
o'er me roll, e-ven when my heart is break-ing,
still is high, storms a-bout me, night o'er-takes me,
him I find, he has grant-ed me for-give-ness,

Refrain

he, my Sav-ior, makes me whole.
he, my Strength, my vic-tory wins.
he, my Com-fort, helps my soul. Hal-le-lu-jah! what a
he, my Pi-lot, hears my cry.
I am his, and he is mine.

WORDS: J. Wilbur Chapman, 1910
MUSIC: Rowland H. Prichard, c. 1830

HYFRYDOL
8.7.8.7.D.

The Service of the Table

Invitation to Communion Songs

❖ ❖ ❖

I Come with Joy   195

1. I come with joy a child of God, for given, loved, and free, the life of Jesus to recall, in love laid down for me.
2. I come with Christians far and near to find, as all are fed, the new communi- ty of love in Christ's communion bread.
3. As Christ breaks bread, and bids us share, each proud division ends. The love that made us, makes us one, and strangers now are friends.
4. The Spirit of the risen Christ, unseen, but ever near, is in such friendship better known, alive among us here.
5. Together met, together bound by all that God has done, we'll go with joy, to give the world, the love that makes us one.

WORDS: Brian Wren, 1970.
MUSIC: American; harm. Annabel Morris Buchanan, 1938
Words © 1971 by Hope Publishing Co., Carol Stream, IL 60188. All Rights Reserved.

LAND OF REST
CM

THE SERVICE OF THE TABLE

196 Love Divine, All Loves Excelling

1. Love divine, all loves excelling, joy of heaven, to earth come down; fix in us thy humble dwelling, all thy faithful mercies crown.
2. Come, Almighty to deliver, let us all thy life receive; suddenly return, and never, nevermore thy temples leave.
3. Finish, then, thy new creation; pure and spotless let us be; let us see thy great salvation perfectly restored in thee:

WORDS: Charles Wesley
MUSIC: Rowland H. Prichard

HYFRYDOL
87 87 D

THE SERVICE OF THE TABLE

197 Come, Let Us Eat

1. Come, let us eat, for now the feast is spread;
2. Come, let us drink, for now the wine is poured;
3. In his pres-ence now we meet and rest,
4. Rise, then, to spread a-broad God's might-y Word;

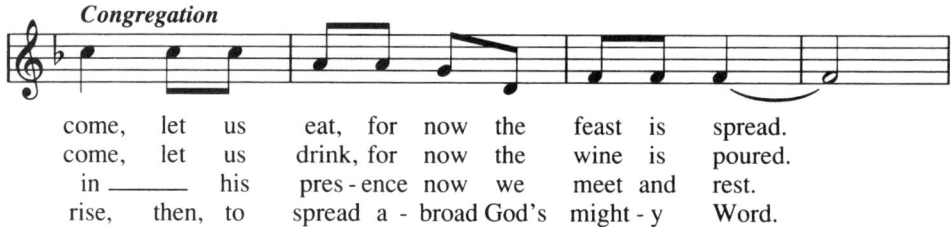

come, let us eat, for now the feast is spread.
come, let us drink, for now the wine is poured.
in his pres-ence now we meet and rest.
rise, then, to spread a-broad God's might-y Word.

Our Lord's bod-y let us take to-geth-er,
Je-sus' blood poured let us drink to-geth-er,
In the pres-ence of our Lord we gath-er,
Je-sus ris-en will bring in the king-dom,

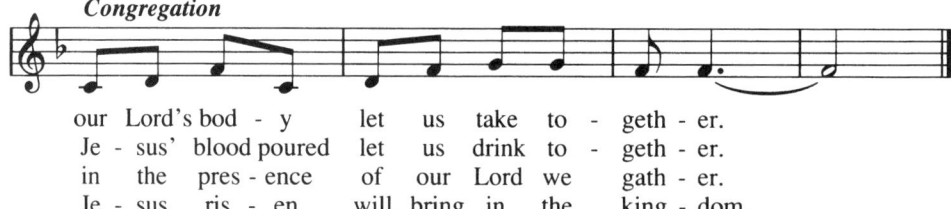

our Lord's bod-y let us take to-geth-er.
Je-sus' blood poured let us drink to-geth-er.
in the pres-ence of our Lord we gath-er.
Je-sus ris-en will bring in the king-dom.

TEXT: st. 1–3, Billema Kwillia, tr. Margaret D. Miller, alt.; st. 4, Gilbert E. Doan, alt.
TUNE: Billema Kwillia, harm. *Contemporary Worship 4*
By kind permission of the Lutheran World Federation.
Text of stanza 4 is reprinted from COMTEMPORARY WORSHIP 4,
copyright © 1972 by permission of Augsburg Fortress.

A VA DE
10 10 10 10

THE SERVICE OF THE TABLE

199 This Is the Feast of Victory

Antiphon

This is the feast of vic-to-ry for our God.

Al-le-lu-ia! Al-le-lu-ia! Al-le-lu-ia!

Leader (Opt. Choir in unison) or Congregation

1. Wor-thy is Christ, the Lamb who was slain, whose
2. Pow - er, rich - es, wis - dom, and strength, and
3. Sing with all the peo - ple of God, and
4. Bless - ing, hon - or, glo - ry, and might be to
5. For the Lamb who was slain has be -

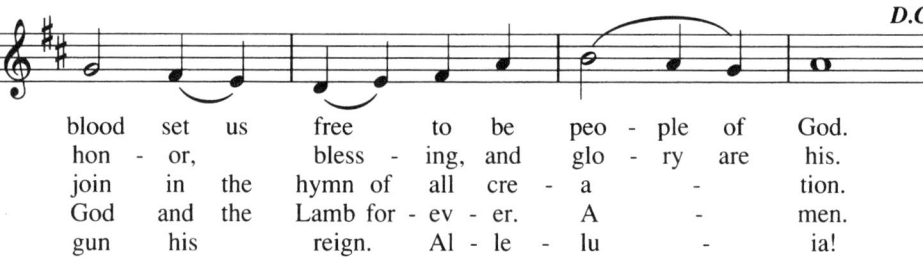

blood set us free to be peo - ple of God.
hon - or, bless - ing, and glo - ry are his.
join in the hymn of all cre - a - tion.
God and the Lamb for - ev - er. A - men.
gun his reign. Al - le - lu - ia!

Final Antiphon

This is the feast of vic-to-ry for our God.

Al-le-lu-ia! Al-le-lu-ia! Al-le-lu - ia!

WORDS: Revelation 5:12–13; trans. by John W. Arthur, 1970
MUSIC: Richard Hillert, 1975, alt.
Text is reprinted from CONTEMPORARY WORSHIP 2, copyright © 1970.
Reprinted by permission of Augsburg Fortress.
Music copyright © 1975, 1988 Richard Hillert.

FESTIVAL CANTICLE
Irregular, with Refrain

INVITATION TO COMMUNION SONGS

Hallelujah, My Father 200

WORDS and MUSIC: Tim Cullen
© 1975 CELEBRATION (Administered by THE COPYRIGHT COMPANY, Nasville, TN)
All Rights Reserved. International Copyright Secured. Used by Permission.

THE SERVICE OF THE TABLE

201 Be Still, for the Spirit of the Lord

1. Be still, for the Spir-it of the Lord, the Ho-ly One, is here.
2. Be still, for the glo-ry of the Lord is shin-ing all a-round;
3. Be still, for the pow-er of the Lord is mov-ing in this place,

Come, bow be-fore Him now, with rev-'rence and with fear.
He burns with ho-ly fire, with splen-dor He is crowned.
He comes to cleanse and heal, to min-is-ter His grace.

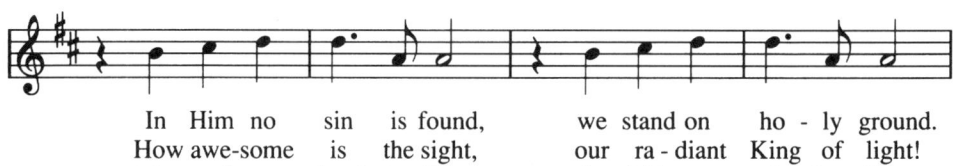

In Him no sin is found, we stand on ho-ly ground.
How awe-some is the sight, our ra-diant King of light!
No work too hard for Him, in faith re-ceive from Him.

Be still, for the Spir-it of the Lord, the Ho-ly One, is here.
Be still, for the glo-ry of the Lord is shin-ing all a-round.
Be still, for the pow-er of the Lord is mov-ing in this place.

WORDS and MUSIC: Dave Evans
© 1982 Make Way Music/Adm. in N., S., & C. America by Integrity's Hosanna! Music.
c/o Integrity Music, Inc., P.O Box 851622, Mobile, AL 36685.
All Rights Reserved. International Copyright Secured. Used by Permission.

INVITATION TO COMMUNION SONGS

Sing Alleluia to the Lord 202

WORDS: St. 1–4, early Christian liturgy; st. 5, Linda Stassen, 1974
MUSIC: Linda Stassen, 1974; harm. Dale Grotenhuis, 1986
© 1974 Linda Stassen, New Song Ministries, R.R. 1, Box 454, Erin, TN 37061.
All Rights Reserved. International Copyright Secured. Used by permission only.

SING ALLELUIA
Irregular

Sanctus Songs

203 Holy Is the Lord

Holy, holy, holy, holy is the Lord.

Holy, holy, holy, holy is the Lord.

Holy is the Father, Holy is the Son,

Holy is the Spirit: blessed Three-in-One.

WORDS: Traditional, based on Isaiah 6:3
MUSIC: Franz Schubert, c. 1826

HOLY IS THE LORD
6.5.6.5.D.

THE SERVICE OF THE TABLE

205 Holy, Holy, Holy Is the Lord of Hosts

Ho - ly, ho - ly, ho - ly is the Lord of hosts.

Ho - ly, ho - ly, ho - ly is the Lord of hosts. The

whole earth is full of His glo - ry, the whole earth is full of His glo - ry, the

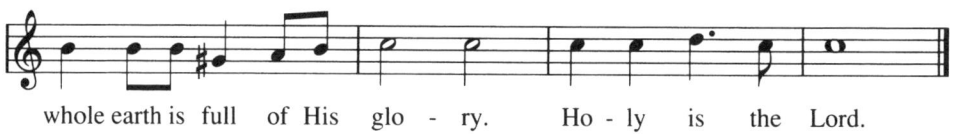
whole earth is full of His glo - ry. Ho - ly is the Lord.

WORDS and MUSIC: Nolene Prince
© 1976 NOLENE PRINCE (Administered by RESOURCE CHRISTIAN MUSIC PTY. LTD.
c/o THE COPYRIGHT COMPANY, Nashville, TN)
All Rights Reserved. International Copyright Secured. Used by Permission.

206 Holy, Holy

1. Ho - ly, ho - ly, ho - ly, ho - ly, ho - ly,
2. Gra - cious Fa - ther, gra - cious Fa - ther, we're so
3. Pre - cious Je - sus, pre - cious Je - sus, we're so
4. Ho - ly Spir - it, Ho - ly Spir - it, come and
5. Hal - le - lu - jah, hal - le - lu - jah, hal - le -

WORDS and MUSIC: Jimmy Owens
© 1972 Bud John Songs, Inc. Admin. by EMI Christian Music Publishing.
All Rights Reserved. Used by Permission.

THE SERVICE OF THE TABLE

207 Holy, Holy, Holy Lord

WORDS: Sanctus
MUSIC: Trad. American Melody, Arr. by Jack Schrader
Arr. © 1995 by Hope Publishing Co.

LAND OF REST
C.M.

SANCTUS SONGS

"Holy, Holy, Holy" 208
"Santo, Santo, Santo"

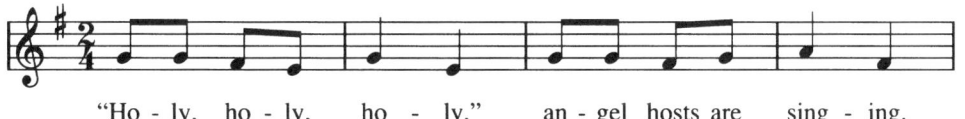

"Ho - ly, ho - ly, ho - ly," an - gel hosts are sing - ing.
"San - to, san - to, san - to," can - tan se - ra - fi - nes.

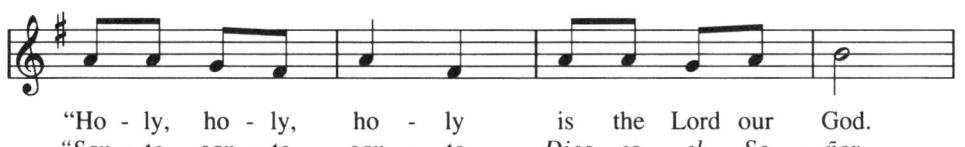

"Ho - ly, ho - ly, ho - ly is the Lord our God.
"San - to, san - to, san - to, Dios es el Se - ñor.

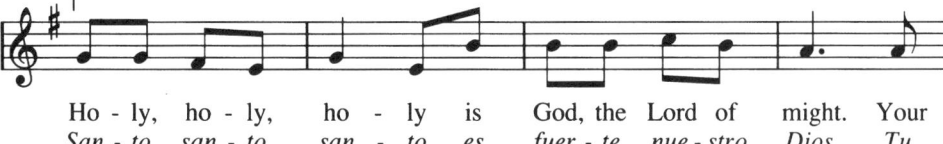

Ho - ly, ho - ly, ho - ly is God, the Lord of might. Your
San - to, san - to, san - to es fuer - te nue - stro Dios. Tu

glo - ry fills the heav - ens, your glo - ry fills the earth." Ho -
glo - ria lle - na los cie - los, la tie - rra lle - na es - tá." Ho -

san - na in the high - est, ho - san - na is our song.
san - na en las al - tu - ras, ho - san - na la can - ción.

WORDS: Isaiah 6:3; English para. Bert Polman, 1985
MUSIC: harmonization AnnaMae Meyer Bush, 1985
Words and harmonization © 1987, CRC Publications, Grand Rapids, MI 49560.
All Rights Reserved. Used by Permission.

MERENGUE

Acclamation Songs

209 Christ Has Died, Christ Is Risen

WORDS: from an ancient liturgy for the Lord's Supper
MUSIC: James A. Kriewald
Music © 1985, The United Methodist Publishing House

210 Christ Has Died

WORDS: from *The Book of Common Prayer*
MUSIC: Betty Pulkingham
Words Copyright 1977 by Charles Mortimer Guilbert as custodian of the Standard Book of Common Prayer.
All Rights Reserved. Reprinted by Permission.
Music © Copyright 1973, by G.I.A. Publications, Inc., 7404 S. Mason Ave., Chicago, Illinois 60638.
International Copyright Secured. All Rights Reserved. Used by Permission.

ACCLAMATION SONGS

We Remember His Death 211

WORDS: from *The Book of Common Prayer*
MUSIC: Betty Pulkingham
Music © 1974 CELEBRATION (Administered by THE COPYRIGHT COMPANY, Nashville, TN)
All Rights Reserved. International Copyright Secured. Used by Permission.

THE SERVICE OF THE TABLE

212 Christ Has Died

*Optional interlude continues.

WORDS: Eucharistic Acclamation, Nos. 1 and 2.
MUSIC: Marty Haugen
© GIA

Lamb of God Songs

214 Lamb of God

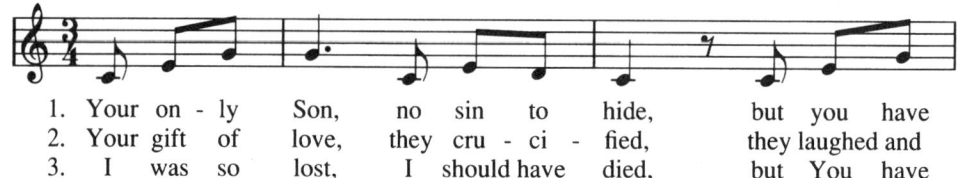

1. Your on-ly Son, no sin to hide, but you have
2. Your gift of love, they cru-ci-fied, they laughed and
3. I was so lost, I should have died, but You have

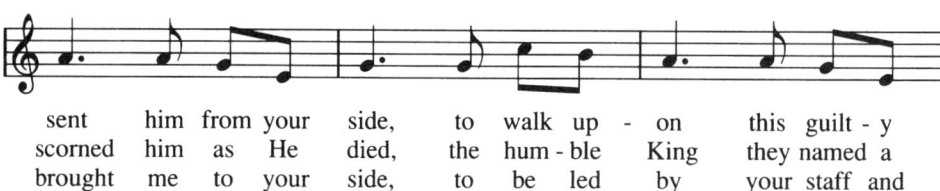

sent him from your side, to walk up-on this guilt-y
scorned him as He died, the hum-ble King they named a
brought me to your side, to be led by your staff and

Refrain

sod, and to be-come the Lamb of God.
fraud, and sac-ri-ficed the Lamb of God. O Lamb of
rod, and to be called a lamb of God.

God, sweet Lamb of God, I love the ho-ly Lamb of God! O wash me

in his pre-cious blood— my Je-sus Christ, the Lamb of God.

WORDS and MUSIC: Twila Paris
© 1985 Straightway Music/Mountain Spring Muisc. Admin. by EMI Christian Music Publishing.
All Rights Reserved. Used by Permission.

LAMB OF GOD SONGS

Jesus, Lamb of God 215

WORDS: *International Consultation on English Texts.*
MUSIC: Betty Pulkingham, from the *Mass for the King of Glory*, © 1974, 1975;
Music © 1974 CELEBRATION (Administered by THE COPYRIGHT COMPANY, Nashville, TN)
All Rights Reserved. International Copyright Secured. Used by Permission.

THE SERVICE OF THE TABLE

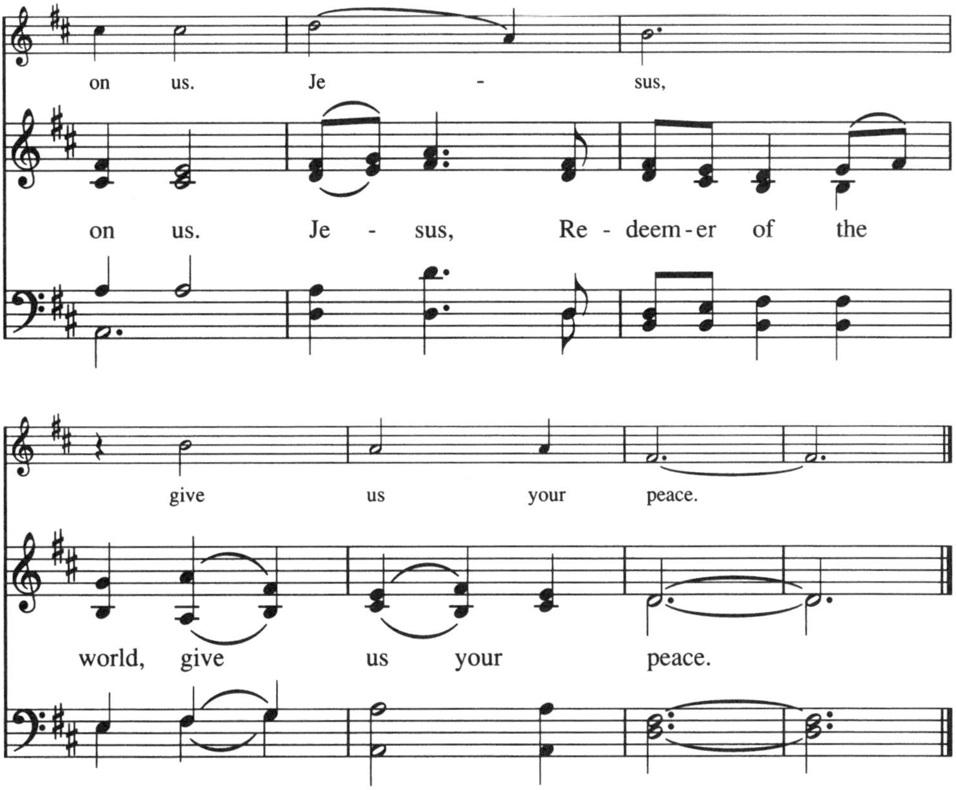

LAMB OF GOD SONGS

O Christ, the Lamb of God 216

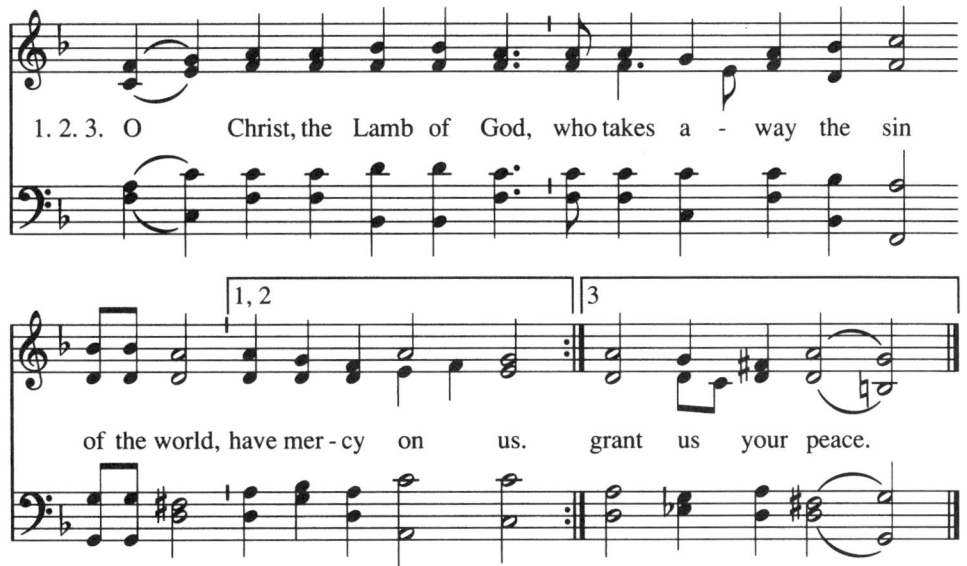

WORDS: Based on John 1:29, *Agnus Dei*
MUSIC: Setting Adapted from Joachim Decker, 1604

Irregular

Communion Songs

217 Gift of Finest Wheat

With simple lyricism

Refrain

You sat-is-fy the hun-gry heart with gift of fin-est wheat; come give to us, O sav-ing Lord, the bread of life to eat. *Fine*

1. As when the shep-herd calls his sheep, they know and heed his voice; so when you call your fam-'ly, Lord, we fol-low and re-joice.
2. With joy-ful lips we sing to you our praise and grat-i-tude, that you should count us wor-thy, Lord, to share this heav'n-ly food.
3. Is not the cup we bless and share the blood of Christ out-poured? Do not one cup, one loaf, de-clare our one-ness in the Lord?
4. The mys-t'ry of your pres-ence, Lord, no mor-tal tongue can tell: whom all the world can-not con-tain comes in our hearts to dwell.
5. You give your-self to us, O Lord; then self-less let us be, to serve each oth-er in your name in truth and char-i-ty.

D.C.

WORDS: Omer Westendorf
MUSIC: Robert E. Kreutz
© Copyright permission obtained, Archdiocese of Philadelphia, 1977. All Rights Reserved.

COMMUNION SONGS

Broken for Me 218

1. Bro-ken for me, bro-ken for you;

the bod-y of Je - sus bro-ken for you.

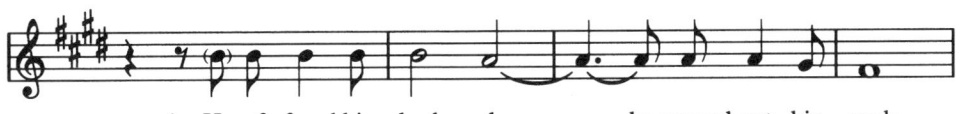

1. He of-fered his bod - dy,   he poured out his soul;
2. Come to my ta - ble   and with me dine;
3. This is my bod - y   giv - en for you;
4. This is my blood   I shed for you,

Je-sus was bro - ken   that we might be whole.
eat of my bread   and drink of my wine.
eat it, re - mem - b'ring   I died for you.
for your for - give - ness,   mak-ing you new.

bro - ken for you.

WORDS and MUSIC: Janet Lunt; Arr. Mimi Farra
© 1978 Sovereign Music UK, P.O. Box 356, Leighton Buzzard, Beds LU7 8WP UK.
All Rights Reserved. Used by Permission.

THE SERVICE OF THE TABLE

219 O the Blood of Jesus

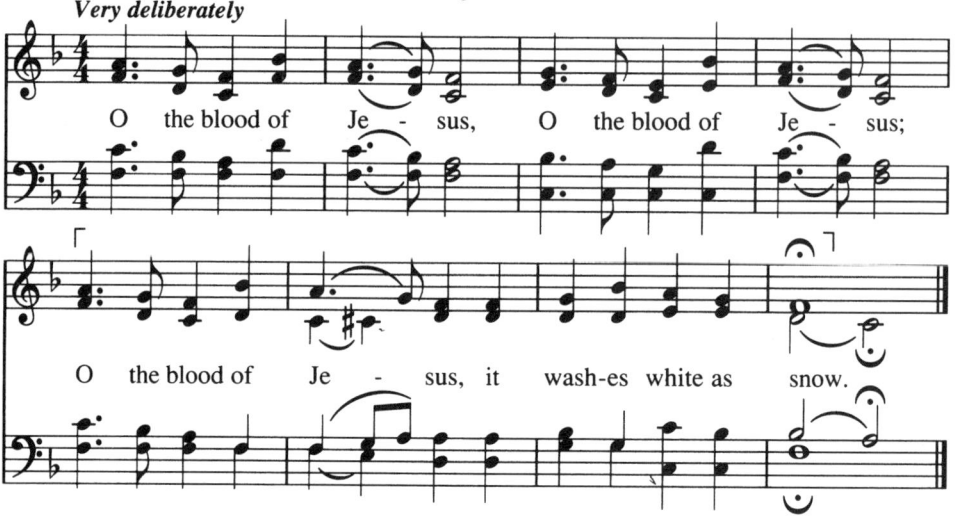

Very deliberately

O the blood of Je-sus, O the blood of Je-sus;
O the blood of Je-sus, it wash-es white as snow.

WORDS and MUSIC: Unknown, Arr. by Jack Schrader
Music arr. © 1995 by Hope Publishing Co., Carol Stream, IL 60188. All Rights Reserved.

220 Let the Hungry Come to Me

1. "Let the hun-gry come to me, let the poor be fed.
   Let the thirst-y come and drink, share my wine and bread.
   Though you have no mon-ey, come to me and eat.
   Drink the cup I of-fer, feed on fin-est wheat.

2. "I my-self am liv-ing bread; feed on me and live.
   In this cup my blood for you; drink the wine I give.
   All who eat my bod-y, all who drink my blood,
   shall have joy for-ev-er, share the life of God.

3. "Here a-mong you shall I dwell; all things new shall be.
   You shall be my ver-y own, I your God with you.
   Bless'd are you in-vit-ed to my wed-ding feast."
   You shall live for-ev-er, all your joys in-creased.

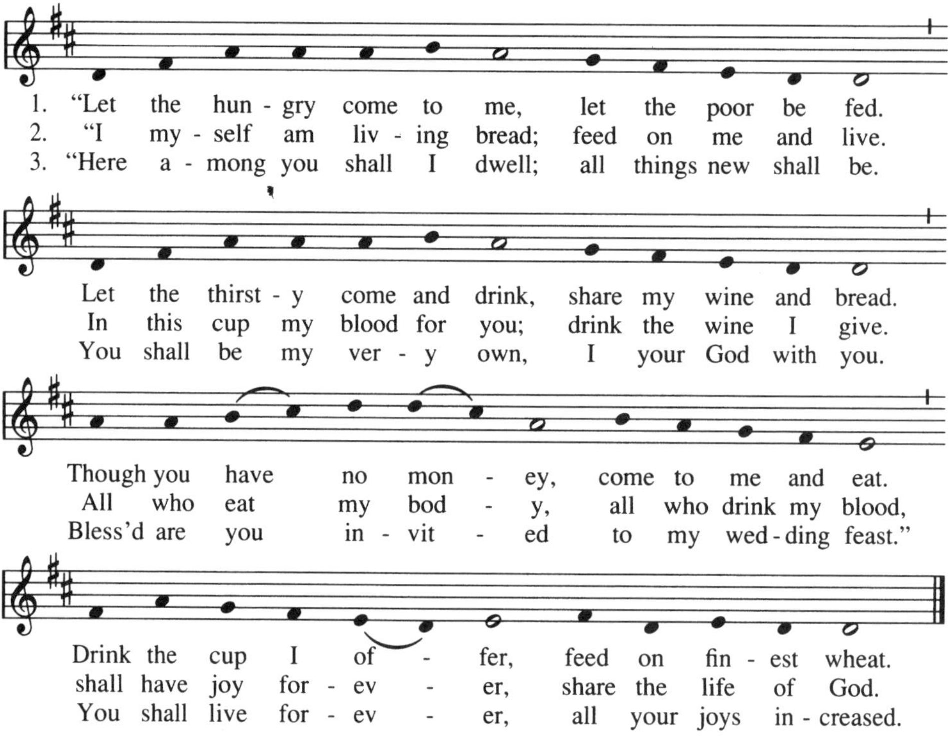

WORDS: Sr. Delores Dufner, OSB
MUSIC: *Processionale*, 1697
Verses from the Gregorian Chant, "Adoro Te Devote," Mode V, with organ accompaniment
by Cecile Gertken, OSB, copyright 1989 by the Sisters of St. Benedict, St. Joseph, MN 56374-0277.

ADORO TE DEVOTE
12.12.11.11.

COMMUNION SONGS

Now the Silence, Then the Glory 221

1. Now the si-lence Now the peace Now the emp-ty hands up-lift-ed
2. Then the glo-ry Then the rest Then the sab-bath peace un-bro-ken

Now the kneel-ing Now the plea Now the Fa-ther's arms in wel-come
Then the gar-den Then the throne Then the crys-tal riv - er flow-ing

Now the hear-ing Now the power Now the ves-sel brimmed for pour-ing
Then the splen-dor Then the life Then the new cre-a - tion sing-ing

Now the bod-y Now the blood Now the joy-ful cel - e-bra-tion
Then the mar-riage Then the love Then the feast of joy un-end-ing

Now the wed-ding Now the songs Now the heart for-giv - en leap-ing
Then the know-ing Then the light Then the ul - ti - mate ad-ven-ture

Now the Spir-it's vis - i - ta - tion Now the Son's e-piph-a-ny
Then the Spir-it's har - vest gath-ered Then the Lamb in maj - es - ty

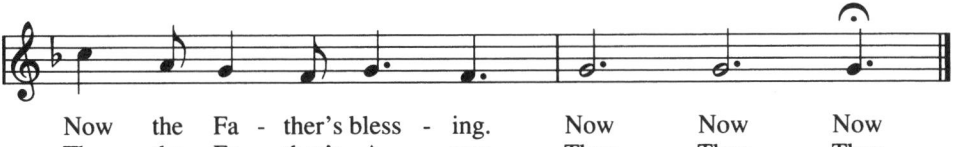

Now the Fa-ther's bless-ing.   Now   Now   Now
Then the Fa-ther's A - men   Then   Then   Then

WORDS: Jaroslav J. Vajda
MUSIC: Carl F. Schalk
Copyright © 1969 by Hope Publishing Co., Carol Stream, IL 60188. All Rights Reserved.

NOW

THE SERVICE OF THE TABLE

222 Seekers of Your Heart

WORDS and MUSIC: Melodie Tunney, Dick Tunney & Beverly Darnall
© 1986 BMG Songs, Inc. (ASCAP)/Pamela Kay Music (Administered by
THE COPYRIGHT COMPANY, Nashville, TN)/BMG Songs, Inc.
All Rights Reserved. International Copyright Secured. Used by Permission.

THE SERVICE OF THE TABLE

223 Soften My Heart

Soften my heart, Lord, soften my heart;
from all indiff'rence set me apart.
To feel your compassion, to weep with your tears;
come soften my heart, O Lord, soften my heart.

WORDS and MUSIC: Graham Kendrick
© 1988 by Make Way Music/Adm. in N., S., & C., America by Integrity's Hosanna! Music.
c/o Integrity Music, Inc., P.O. Box 851622, Mobile, AL 36685.
All Rights Reserved. International Copyright Secured. Used by Permission

224 Healer of My Soul

1. Healer of my soul, keep me at evening.
   Keep me at morning, keep me at noon, healer of my soul.
2. Keeper of my soul, on rough course faring.
   Help and safeguard my means this night, keeper of my

WORDS and MUSIC: John Michael Talbot
© 1983 Birdwing Music/Cherry Lane Music Publishing Co., Inc.
Admin. by EMI Christian Music Publishing.
All Rights Reserved. Used by Permission.

COMMUNION SONGS

soul. I am tired a-stray and stum-bling,

shield my soul from the snare of sin.

I Will Change Your Name 225

I will change your name, you shall no
I will change your name, your new

long-er be called wound-ed,
name shall be con-fi-dence,

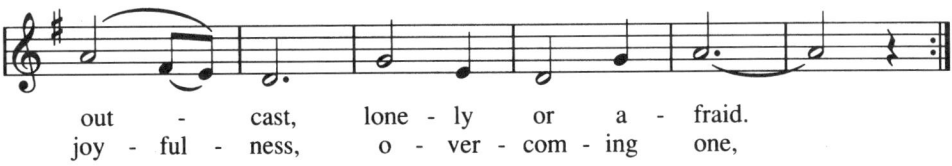
out-cast, lone-ly or a-fraid.
joy-ful-ness, o-ver-com-ing one,

faith-ful-ness, friend of God,

one who seeks my face.

WORDS and MUSIC: D. J. Butler
© 1987 by Mercy Publishing
All Rights Reserved. Used by Permission.

THE SERVICE OF THE TABLE

226 Ubi caritas et amor

*Translation: Where charity and love are found, God is there.
**Choose either part.

WORDS: *Ubi caritas et amor*, 9th c.
MUSIC: Jacques Berthier
Copyright © by Les Presses de Taizé (France). Used by permission of G.I.A. Publications, Inc., Chicago, Illinois, exclusive agent. All Rights Reserved.

UBI CARITAS
Irregular

COMMUNION SONGS

4. Let us be one in love to-geth-er in the one bread of Christ.

5. The love of God in Je-sus Christ bears e-ter-nal joy.

6. The love of God in Je-sus Christ will nev-er have an end.

*Choose either part.

Jesus, Remember Me 227

Je-sus, re-mem-ber me when you come in-to your King-dom.

Je-sus, re-mem-ber me when you come in-to your King-dom.

(Repeat as needed)

WORDS: Luke 23:42
MUSIC: From the Taizé Community
Copyright © 1981 by Les Presses de Taizé (France). Used by permission of G.I.A. Publications, Inc., Chicago, Illinois, exclusive agent. All Rights Reserved.

THE SERVICE OF THE TABLE

228 Eat This Bread

WORDS: John 6
MUSIC: From the Taizé Community
Copyright © 1984 by Les Presses de Taizé (France). Used by permission of G.I.A. Publications, Inc.,
Chicago, Illinois, exclusive agent. All Rights Reserved.

COMMUNION SONGS

Let All Mortal Flesh Keep Silence 229

WORDS: *Liturgy of St. James*, 4th C.; adapt. Gerard Moultrie, 1864
MUSIC: Traditional French melody, 17th C.; harm. *English Hymnal*, 1906

PICARDY
8.7.8.7.8.7.

THE SERVICE OF THE TABLE

230 O Christe Domine Jesu
O Christ, Lord Jesus

Refrain *In Harmony*

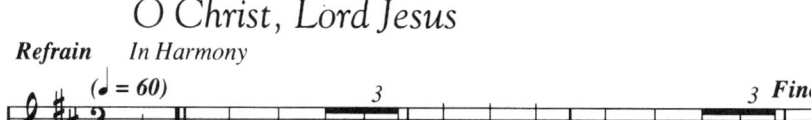

O Chri-ste Do-mi-ne Je-su, O Chri-ste Do-mi-ne Je-su! O

Verses
Leader

1. The Lord is my shep-herd; there is noth-ing I shall want.

Fresh and green are the pas-tures where he gives me re-pose. Near

rest-ful wa-ters he leads me to re-vive my droop-ing spir-it.

He guides me a-long the right path; he is true to his name. If I should

walk in the val-ley of dark-ness no e-vil would I fear.

2. You are there with your rod and staff; with these you give me com-fort.

WORDS: Psalm 23
MUSIC: From the Taizé Community
Copyright © 1984 by Les Presses de Taizé (France). Used by permission of G.I.A. Publications, Inc., Chicago, Illinois, exclusive agent. All Rights Reserved.

COMMUNION SONGS

You have pre-pared a ban-quet for me in the sight of my foes.

My head you have a-nointed with oil; my cup is o-ver-flow-ing. Sure-ly

good-ness and kind-ness shall fol-low me all the days of my life.

In the Lord's own house shall I dwell for ev - er and ev - er.

*Choose either part.

How Blessed Are You 231

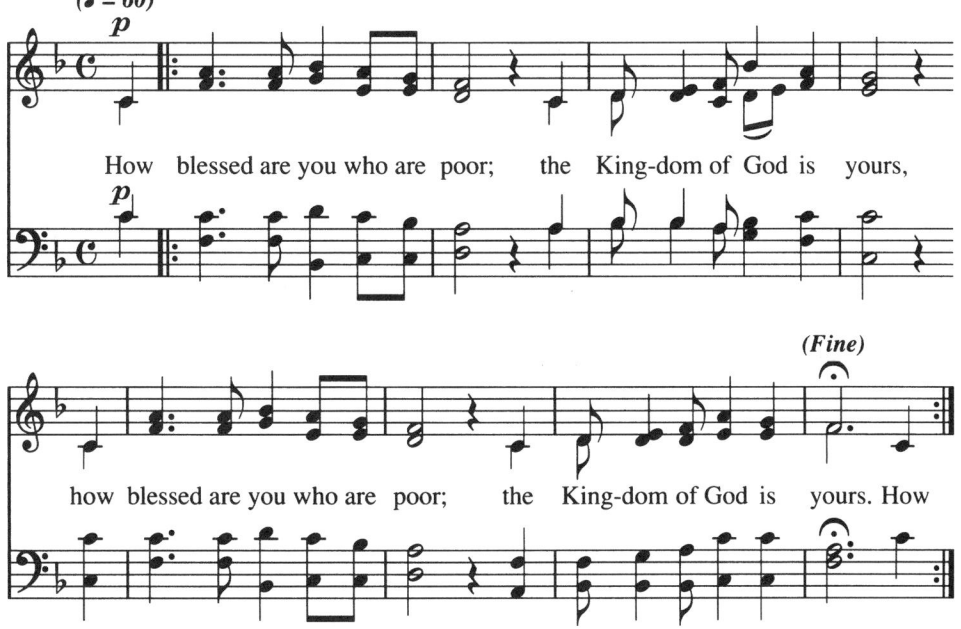

How blessed are you who are poor; the King-dom of God is yours,

how blessed are you who are poor; the King-dom of God is yours. How

WORDS: Matt:5
MUSIC: From the Taizé Community
Copyright © by Les Presses de Taizé (France). Used by permission of G.I.A. Publications, Inc.,
Chicago, Illinois, exclusive agent. All Rights Reserved.

THE SERVICE OF THE TABLE

232 There Is a Redeemer

1. There is a Re-deem-er, Je-sus, God's own Son,
2. Je-sus, my Re-deem-er, name a-bove all names,
3. When I stand in glo-ry I will see His face, and

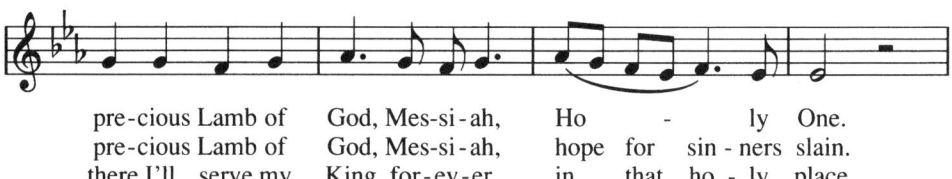

pre-cious Lamb of God, Mes-si-ah, Ho - ly One.
pre-cious Lamb of God, Mes-si-ah, hope for sin-ners slain.
there I'll serve my King for-ev-er, in that ho-ly place.

Thank you, O my Fa - ther, for giv-ing us your Son; and

leav - ing your Spir - it 'til the work on earth is done.

WORDS and MUSIC: Keith Green
© 1982 Birdwing Music/Cherry Lane Music Publishing Co., Inc./Ears to Hear Music.
Admin. by EMI Christian Music Publishing. All Rights Reserved. Used by Permission.

COMMUNION SONGS

Glory Be to Jesus 233

With breadth

1. Glo-ry be to Je - sus, who in bit-ter pains
2. Grace and life e - ter - nal in that blood I find.
3. Blest through end-less a - ges be the pre-cious stream

poured for me the life blood from his sa-cred veins!
Blest be his com - pas - sion in - fi - nite-ly kind!
which from sin and sor - row doth the world re - deem!

WORDS: Tr. Edward Caswall
MUSIC: Friedrick Filitz
Music descant © 1965 CELEBRATION (Administered by THE COPYRIGHT COMPANY, Nashville, TN)
All Rights Reserved. International Copyright Secured. Used by Permission.

CASWALL

THE SERVICE OF THE TABLE

234 Worthy Is the Lamb

WORDS: Revelations 5:12, adapt. Don Wyrtzen, 1973
MUSIC: Don Wyrtzen, 1973
Copyright © 1973 Singspiration Music/ASCAP. All Rights Reserved.
Used by permission of Benson Music Group, Inc.

WORTHY IS THE LAMB
Irregular

COMMUNION SONGS

O Sacred Head, Now Wounded 235

1. O sacred head, now wounded, with grief and shame weighed down,
now scornfully surrounded with thorns, thine only crown:
O sacred head, what glory, what bliss till now was thine;
yet, though despised and gory, I joy to call thee mine.

2. What thou, my Lord, hast suffered was all for sinners' gain;
mine, mine was the transgression, but thine the deadly pain.
Lo, here I fall, my Savior! 'Tis I deserve thy place;
look on me with thy favor, and grant to me thy grace.

3. What language shall I borrow to thank thee, dearest friend,
for this thy dying sorrow, thy pity without end?
O make me thine forever; and should I fainting be,
Lord, let me never, never outlive my love to thee.

WORDS: Attr. Bernard of Clairvaux, 12th C.; tr. (German) Paul Gerhardt, 1656;
tr. (English) James W. Alexander, 1830
MUSIC: Hans Leo Hassler, 1601; arr. J. S. Bach, 1729

PASSION CHORALE
7.6.7.6.D.

COMMUNION SONGS

Jesus, Stand Among Us 237

1. Jesus, stand among us in your risen power;
   let this time of worship be a hallowed hour. A-men.
2. Breathe the Holy Spirit into every heart;
   bid the fears and sorrows from each soul depart. A-men.

WORDS: William Pennefather, 1873
MUSIC: Friedrich Filitz, 1847

BEMERTON
6.5.6.5.

Post-Communion Songs

238 He Is Exalted

($\quarternote = 62$)

He is ex-alt-ed the King is ex-alt-ed on high; I will praise him. He is ex-alt-ed for-ev-er ex-alt-ed and I will praise his name! He is the Lord, for-ev-er his truth shall reign; hea-ven and earth re-joice in his Ho-ly name. He is ex-alt-ed, the King is ex-alt-ed on high.

WORDS and MUSIC: Twila Paris
Copyright © 1985 Straightway Music. Admin. by Gaither Music Management
All Rights Reserved. International Copyright Secured. Used by Permission

239 Hallelujah! We Sing Your Praises

Refrain

Hal-le-lu-jah! We sing your prais-es, all our

WORDS and MUSIC: South African
Copyright © 1984 Utryck. Used by permission of Walton Music Corporation.

HALELUYA! PELO TSO RONA
Irregular

POST-COMMUNION SONGS

hearts are filled with glad - ness. Hal - le - lu - jah! We sing your prais - es, all our hearts are filled with glad - ness.

1. Christ the Lord to us said: I am wine, I am bread, I am wine, I am bread, give to all who thirst and hun - ger.
2. Now he sends us all out, strong in faith, free of doubt, strong in faith, free of doubt. Tell to all the joy - ful Gos - pel.

Refrain (after repeat)

THE SERVICE OF THE TABLE

240 Dona Nobis Pacem
(A Round for Peace)

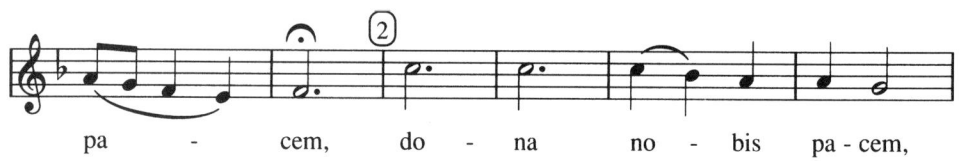

*Translation: "Give us peace."

WORDS and MUSIC: Traditional
© Novello & Co., Ltd., 8/9 Frith Street, London

241 Dona Nobis Pacem Domine

WORDS: Traditional
MUSIC: Jacques Berthier and the Taizé Community
Music copyright © 1982, 1983, 1984 by Les Presses de Taizé (France).
Used by permission of G.I.A. Publications, Inc.,
Chicago, Illinois, exclusive agent. All Rights Reseved.

THE SERVICE OF THE TABLE

243 Be Not Afraid

Verse 1

1. You shall cross the bar-ren des-ert but you

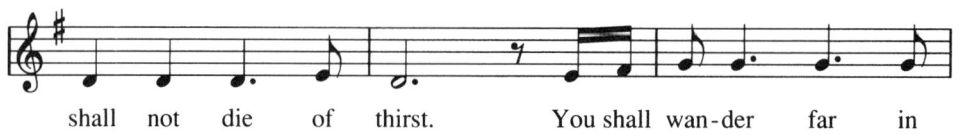
shall not die of thirst. You shall wan-der far in

safe-ty though you do not know the way. You shall

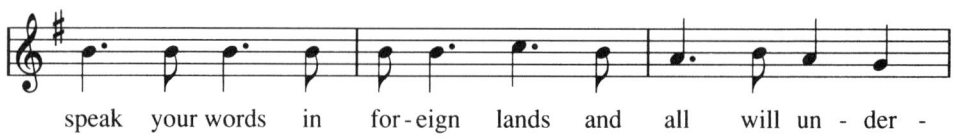
speak your words in for-eign lands and all will un-der-

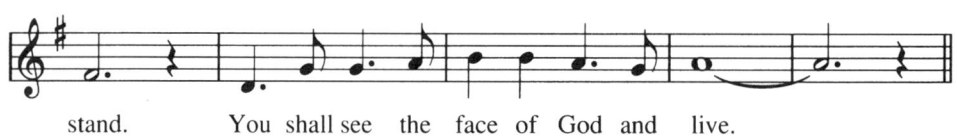
stand. You shall see the face of God and live.

Refrain

Be not a-fraid. I go be-fore you al-ways.

Come, fol-low me, and I will give you rest.

WORDS and MUSIC: Robert J. Dufford
© 1975, 1978, Robert J. Dufford, SJ and New Dawn Music, 5536 NE Hassalo, Portland, OR 97213.
All Rights Reserved. Used by Permission.

POST-COMMUNION SONGS

Verse 2
2. If you pass through rag-ing wa-ters in the sea, you shall not

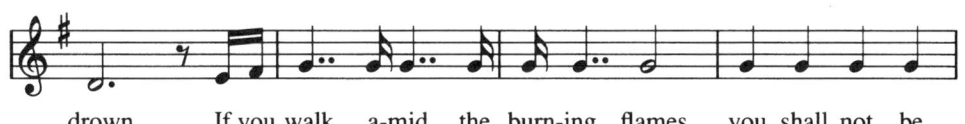
drown. If you walk a-mid the burn-ing flames, you shall not be

harmed. If you stand be-fore the pow'r of hell and death is at your

To Refrain
side, know that I am with you through it all.

Verse 3
3. Bless-ed are your poor, for the king-dom shall be theirs.

Blest are you that weep and mourn, for one day you shall laugh. And if

wick-ed tongues in-sult and hate you all be-cause of me,

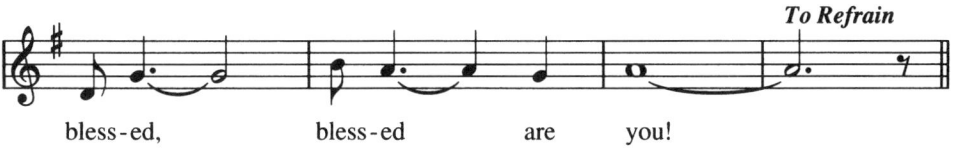
To Refrain
bless-ed, bless-ed are you!

THE SERVICE OF THE TABLE

244 The Battle Belongs to the Lord

1. In heav-en-ly ar-mor we'll en-ter the land, the
2. When the pow-er of dark-ness comes in like a flood, the

bat-tle be-longs to the Lord! No wea-pon that's fash-ioned a-gainst
bat-tle be-longs to the Lord! He's raised up a stand-ard, the power

us will stand, the bat-tle be-longs to the Lord!
of his blood, the bat-tle be-longs to the Lord!

Refrain

We sing glo - ry, hon - or, pow-er and strength to the Lord!

We sing glo - ry, hon - or, pow-er and strength to the Lord!

WORDS and MUSIC: Jamie Owens-Collins, 1984; arr. Robert F. Douglas, 1986
© 1984 Fairhill Music. All Rights Reserved. Used by Permission.

THE BATTLE
11.8.11.8.Refrain

POST-COMMUNION SONGS

Awesome God 245

Our God is an awe-some God, He reigns from heav-en a-bove with wis - dom,

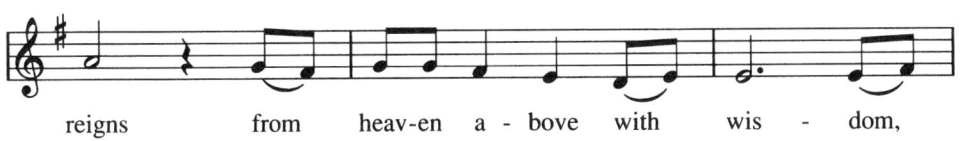

pow'r and love— Our God is an awe-some God! Our

God! Our God is an awe-some God! Our

God is an awe - some God!

WORDS and MUSIC: Rich Mullins
© 1988 BMG Songs, Inc. All Rights Reserved. Used by Permission.

THE SERVICE OF THE TABLE

246 I Am the Bread of Life

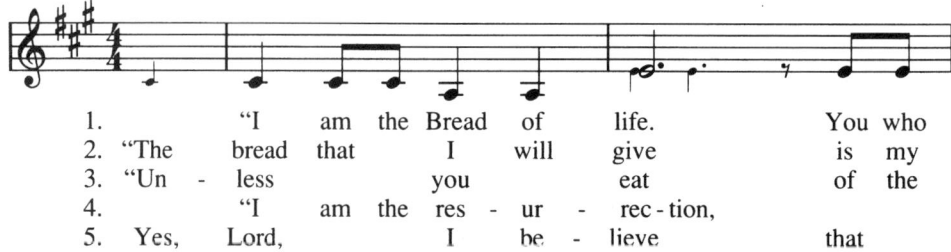

1. "I am the Bread of life. You who
2. "The bread that I will give is my
3. "Un - less you eat of the
4. "I am the res - ur - rec - tion,
5. Yes, Lord, I be - lieve that

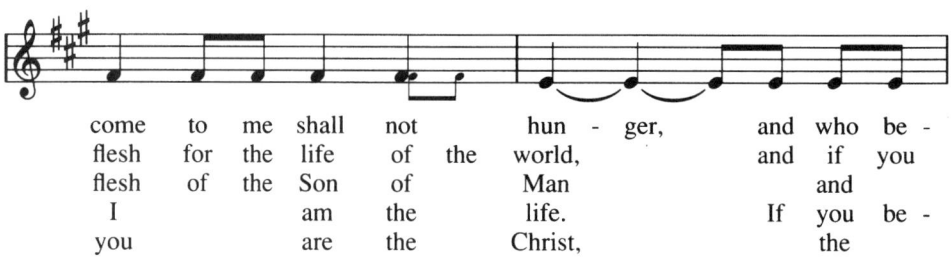

come to me shall not hun - ger, and who be -
flesh for the life of the world, and if you
flesh of the Son of Man and
I am the life. If you be -
you are the Christ, the

lieve in me shall not thirst. No one can come to
eat of this bread, you shall live for -
drink of his blood, and drink of his
lieve in me, e - ven though you
Son of God, who has

me un - less the Fa - ther beck - ons."
ev - er, you shall live for - ev - er."
blood, you shall not have life with - in you."
die, you shall live for - ev - er."
come in - to the world.

WORDS: John 6, adapt. S. Suzanne Toolan
MUSIC: S. Suzanne Toolan
Copyright © 1966 by G.I.A. Publications, Inc., Chicago, Illinois.
All Rights Reseved. Used by Permission.

I AM THE BREAD
Irregular

POST-COMMUNION SONGS

THE SERVICE OF THE TABLE

247 Shine, Jesus, Shine

WORDS and MUSIC: Graham Kendrick
© 1987 Make Way Music/Adm. in N., S., & C. America by Integrity's Hosanna! Music
c/o Integrity Music, Inc., P.O. Box 851622, Mobile, AL 36685
All Rights Reserved. International Copyright Secured. Used by Permission.

THE SERVICE OF THE TABLE

248 Spirit Song

WORDS and MUSIC: John Wimber
© 1980 Mercy Publishing

Praise and Thanksgiving

Songs for Praising the Father

249 Great Is Thy Faithfulness

1. Great is thy faithfulness, O God my Father, there is no shadow of turning with thee; thou changest not, thy compassions they fail not; as thou hast been thou forever wilt be.
2. Summer and winter, and springtime and harvest, sun, moon and stars in their courses above join with all nature in manifold witness to thy great faithfulness, mercy and love.
3. Pardon for sin and a peace that endureth, thy own dear presence to cheer and to guide; strength for today and bright hope for tomorrow, blessings all mine, with ten thousand beside!

WORDS: Thomas O. Chisholm, 1923
MUSIC: William M. Runyan, 1923
Copyright © 1923, renewal 1951 by Hope Publishing Co., Carol Stream, IL 60188. All Rights Reserved.

FAITHFULNESS
11.10.11.10.Ref.

PRAISE AND THANKSGIVING

250 How Great Thou Art

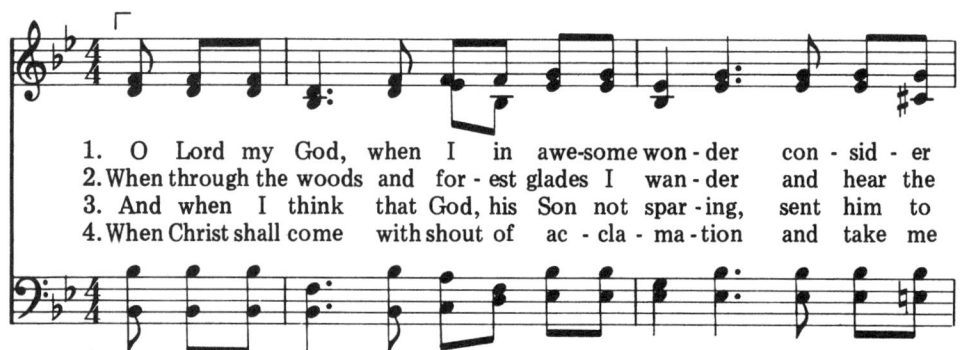

1. O Lord my God, when I in awe-some won-der con-sid-er
2. When through the woods and for-est glades I wan-der and hear the
3. And when I think that God, his Son not spar-ing, sent him to
4. When Christ shall come with shout of ac-cla-ma-tion and take me

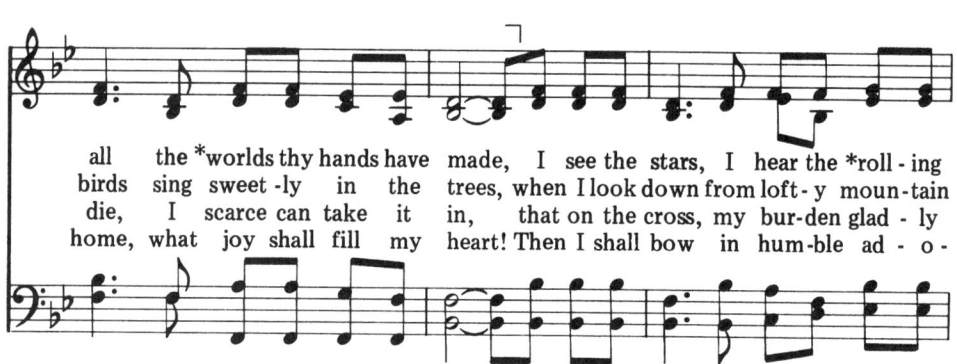

all the *worlds thy hands have made, I see the stars, I hear the *roll-ing
birds sing sweet-ly in the trees, when I look down from loft-y moun-tain
die, I scarce can take it in, that on the cross, my bur-den glad-ly
home, what joy shall fill my heart! Then I shall bow in hum-ble ad-o-

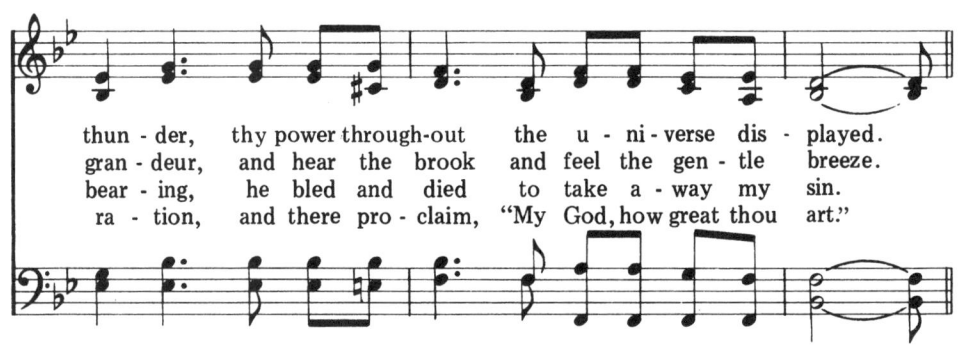

thun-der, thy power through-out the u-ni-verse dis-played.
gran-deur, and hear the brook and feel the gen-tle breeze.
bear-ing, he bled and died to take a-way my sin.
ra-tion, and there pro-claim, "My God, how great thou art."

*Author's original words are "works" and "mighty."

WORDS: Stuart K. Hine, 1949, alt.
MUSIC: Swedish folk melody; arr. Stuart K. Hine, 1949
© Copyright 1953, renewed 1981 by MANNA MUSIC, INC., 35255 Brooten Road, Pacific City, OR 97135.
All Rights Reserved. Used by Permission.

O STORE GUD
11.10.11.10.Ref.

PRAISE AND THANKSGIVING

254 Ah, Lord God

Ah, Lord God, you have made the heav-ens and the earth by your great

pow-er. Ah, Lord God, you have made the heav-ens and the

earth by your out-stretched arm. Noth-ing is too dif-fi-cult for

you, noth-ing is too dif-fi-cult for you. Great and might-y God,

great in coun-sel and might-y in deed. Noth-ing, noth-ing,

ab-so-lute-ly noth-ing, noth-ing is too dif-fi-cult for you.

WORDS and MUSIC: Kay Chance
© 1976 by Kay Chance Dr. H.-Jasper-Str. 20 D-37581 Bad Gandersheim Germany

PRAISING THE FATHER

Give to Our God Immortal Praise 255

1. Give to our God immortal praise; mercy and
2. He built the earth, he spread the sky, and fixed the
3. He fills the sun with morning light; he bids the
4. He sent His Son with power to save from guilt and
5. Through this vast world he guides our feet, and leads us

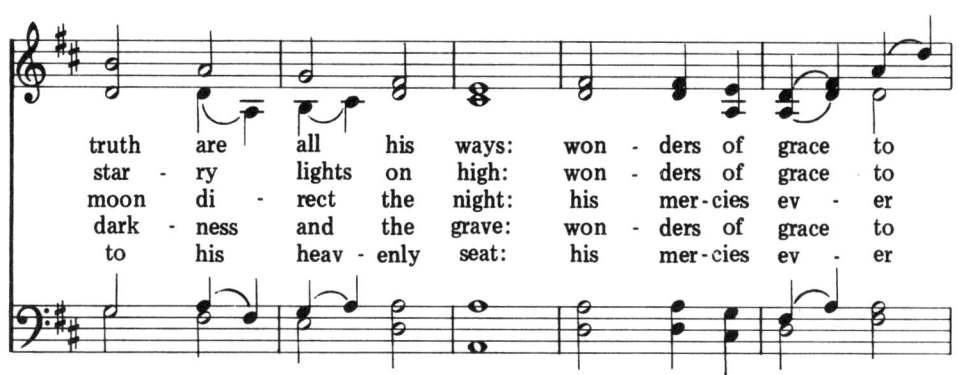

truth are all his ways: wonders of grace to
starry lights on high: wonders of grace to
moon direct the night: his mercies ever
darkness and the grave: wonders of grace to
to his heavenly seat: his mercies ever

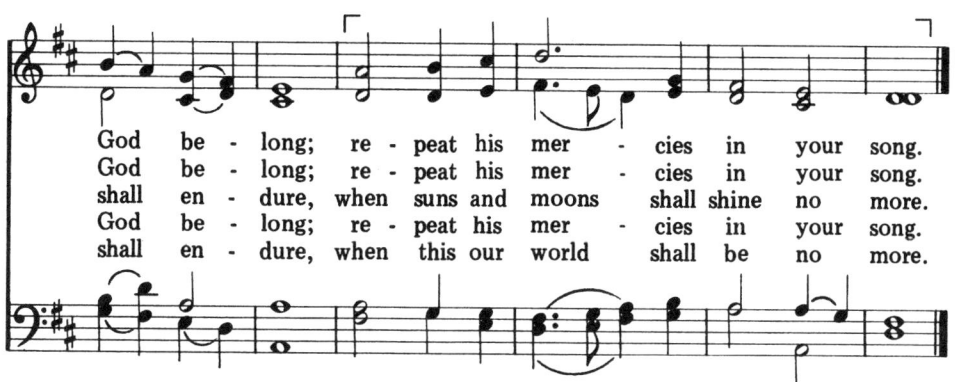

God belong; repeat his mercies in your song.
God belong; repeat his mercies in your song.
shall endure, when suns and moons shall shine no more.
God belong; repeat his mercies in your song.
shall endure, when this our world shall be no more.

WORDS: Isaac Watts, 1719, para. of Ps. 136
MUSIC: John Hatton, 1793

DUKE STREET
L.M.

PRAISE AND THANKSGIVING

256 Sing of the Lord's Goodness

1. Sing of the Lord's good-ness, Fa-ther of all wis-dom,
2. Pow-er he has wield-ed, hon-or is his gar-ment,
3. Cour-age in our dark-ness, com-fort in our sor-row,
4. Praise him with your sing-ing, praise him with the trum-pet,

come to him and bless his name. Mer-cy he has shown us,
ris-en from the snares of death. His word he has spo-ken,
Spi-rit of our God most high; sol-ace for the wea-ry,
praise God with the lute and harp; praise him with the cym-bals,

his love is for-ev-er, faith-ful to the end of days:
one bread he has bro-ken, new life he now gives to all:
par-don for the sin-ner, splen-dor of the liv-ing God:
praise him with your danc-ing, praise God till the end of days:

Chorus

Come, then, all you na-tions, sing of your Lord's good-ness, me-lo-dies of praise and

thanks to God. Ring out the Lord's glo-ry, praise him with your mu-sic,

Last time

wor-ship him and bless his name.

WORDS and MUSIC: Ernest Sands
Arr. Paul Inwood
Words © 1981 Ernest Sands, St Thomas More Group, 30 North Terrace, Mildenhall, Suffolk.
Music arr: © 1986 Paul Inwood. Administered in the UK by the St Thomas More Group

PRAISING THE FATHER

Praise to You, O God of Mercy   257
Thanks Be to You

1. Praise to you, O God of mer-cy! Thanks be to you for-ev-er!
2. From of old you loved and sought us! Thanks be to you for-ev-er!
3. Praise to you, O God of mer-cy! Thanks be to you for-ev-er!

3rd time to Coda

Rais-ing high the weak and low-ly: thanks be to you for-ev-er!
Truth and jus-tice you have taught us: thanks be to you for- ev-er!
Rais-ing high the weak and low-ly: thanks be to you for-

Strong is your faith-ful-ness, strong is your love, re-

to stanza 3

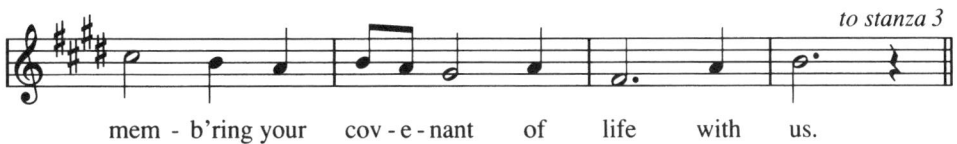

mem-b'ring your cov-e-nant of life with us.

⊕ CODA

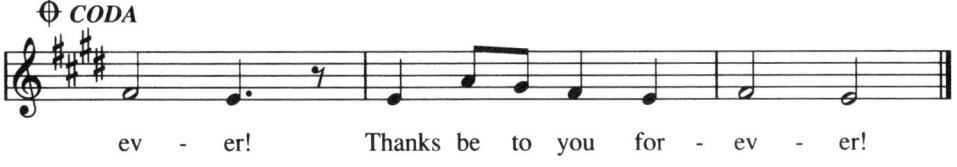

ev-er! Thanks be to you for-ev-er!

WORDS and MUSIC: Marty Haugen
Copyright © 1990 by G.I.A. Publications, Inc., Chicago, Illinois.
All Rights Reserved. Used by Permission.

THANKS BE TO YOU
Irregular

PRAISE AND THANKSGIVING

258 To God Be the Glory

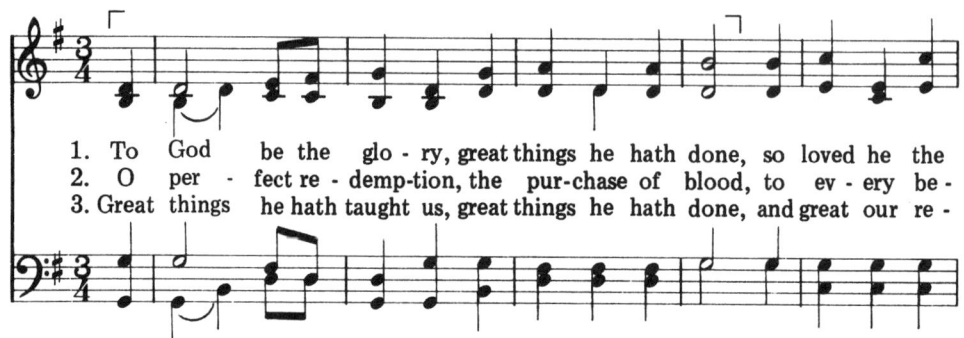

1. To God be the glory, great things he hath done, so loved he the
2. O perfect redemption, the purchase of blood, to every be-
3. Great things he hath taught us, great things he hath done, and great our re-

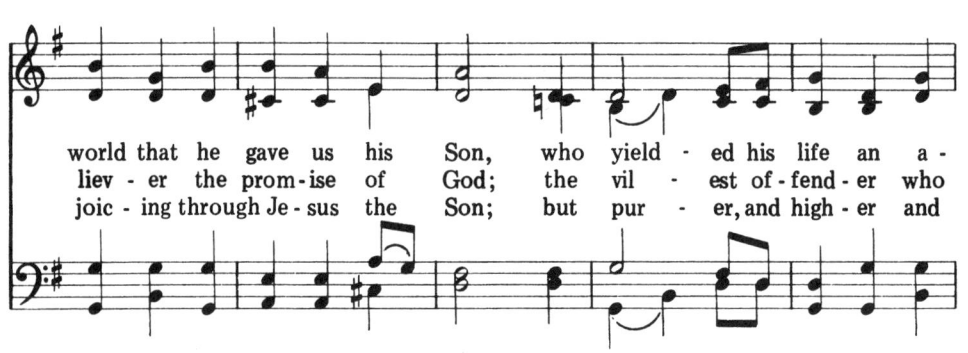

world that he gave us his Son, who yielded his life an a-
liever the promise of God; the vilest offender who
joicing through Jesus the Son; but purer, and higher and

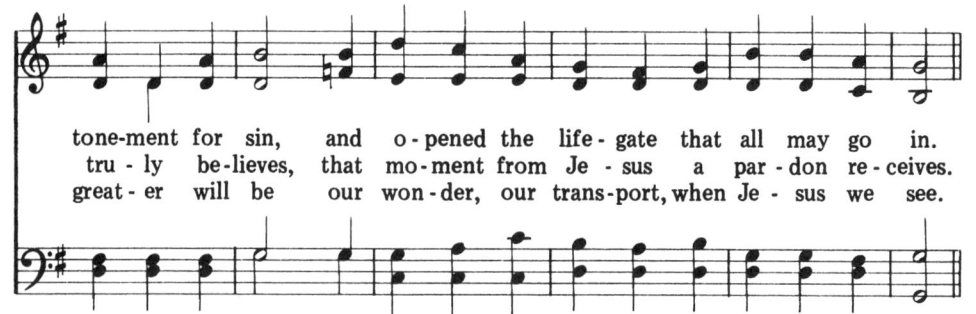

tonement for sin, and opened the life-gate that all may go in.
truly believes, that moment from Jesus a pardon receives.
greater will be our wonder, our transport, when Jesus we see.

WORDS: Fanny J. Crosby, 1875, alt.
MUSIC: William H. Doane, 1875

TO GOD BE THE GLORY
11.11.11.11.Ref.

PRAISING THE FATHER

PRAISE AND THANKSGIVING

260 Blessed Be the Name of the Lord

WORDS and MUSIC: Don Moen
© 1986 by Integrity's Hosanna! Music. c/o Integrity Music, Inc., P.O. Box 851622, Mobile, AL 36685.
All Rights Reserved. International Copyright Secured. Used by Permission.

PRAISING THE FATHER

There's No God As Great 261
No Hay Dios tan Grande

1. There's no god as great as you, O Lord, O Lord, my God.
2. *No hay dios tan gran-de co-mo tú, no lo hay, no lo hay.*

There's no god who works the might-y won-ders, all the won-ders that you
No hay dios que pue-da ha-cer las o - bras co-mo las que ha-ces

do. do. Not by our weap-ons, nor by our pow - er, but by your
tú. tú. No es con es - pa - da, ni con e - jér-ci-to, mas con tu

Spir-it we are led. Not by our weap-ons, nor by our pow - er,
San-to Es-pí - ri - tú. No es con es - pa - da, ni con e - jér-ci-to,

but by your Spir-it we are led. The Ho-ly Spir-it will move the
mas con tu San-to Es-pí - ri - tú. Y es-ta i - gle-sia se mo-ve-

church, the Ho-ly Spir - it will move the church, the Ho-ly
rá, y es-ta i - gle - sia se mo-ve - rá, y es-ta i-

Spir-it will move the church, for by your Spir-it we are led.
gle-sia se mo-ve-rá y con tu San-to Es-pí - ri - tú.

WORDS and MUSIC: Traditional Spanish   NO HAY DIOS

PRAISE AND THANKSGIVING

262 Through Our God We Shall Do Valiantly

Through our God, we shall do val-iant-ly, it is

he who will tread down our en - e-mies, we'll sing and shout his

3rd time to Coda
vic - to - ry, Christ is King! For God has won the

vic - to - ry and set his peo-ple free, his Word has slain the

Repeat twice
en - e - my. The earth shall stand and see that through our

Coda
Christ is King, Christ is King, Christ is King!

WORDS and MUSIC: Dale Garratt
© 1979 SCRIPTURE IN SONG, DIV. INTEGRITY MUSIC (Administered by
MARANATHA! MUSIC c/o THE COPYRIGHT COMPANY, Nasville, TN)
All Rights Reserved. International Copyright Secured. Used by Permission.

PRAISING THE FATHER

Rock of My Salvation 263

WORDS and MUSIC: Teresa Muller
© 1982 MARANATHA! MUSIC (Administered by THE COPYRIGHT COMPANY, Nashville, TN)
All Rights Reserved. International Copyright Secured. Used by Permission.

PRAISE AND THANKSGIVING

264 Abba Father

"Ab-ba Fa-ther; Ab-ba Fa-ther,"

Deep with-in my soul I cry.

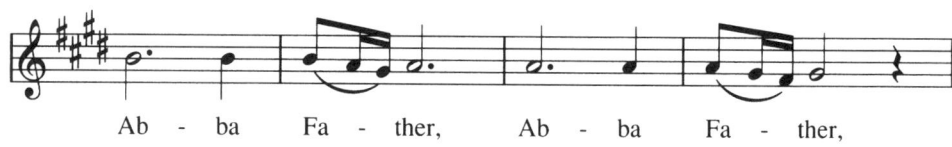
Ab-ba Fa-ther, Ab-ba Fa-ther,

I will nev-er cease to love You.

WORDS and MUSIC: Steve Fry
© 1979 Birdwing Music/Cherry Lane Music Publishing Co., Inc.
Admin. by EMI Christian Music Publishing. All Rights Reserved. Used by Permission.

PRAISING THE FATHER

To Him Who Sits on the Throne 265

To Him who sits on the throne and un-to the Lamb,

to Him who sits on the throne and un-to the Lamb;

be bless-ing and glo-ry and hon-or and pow-er for - ev - er,

be bless-ing and glo-ry and hon-or and pow-er for - ev - er.

WORDS: Debbye Graafsma, Based on Rev. 5:13
MUSIC: Debbye Graafsma
© 1984 by Integrity's Hosanna! Music. c/o Integrity Music, Inc., P.O. Box 851622, Mobile, AL 36685.
All Rights Reserved. International Copyright Secured. Used by Permission.

Songs to Remember the Work of the Son

✣ ✣ ✣

266 Give Thanks with a Grateful Heart

Give thanks with a grateful heart, give thanks to the Holy One, give thanks because he's given Jesus Christ his Son. Give Son. And now let the weak say "I am strong"; let the poor say "I am rich" because of what the Lord has done for

WORDS and MUSIC: Henry Smith, 1978
© 1978 by Integrity's Hosanna! Music, c/o Integrity Music, Inc., P.O. Box 851622, Mobile, AL 36685.
All Rights Reserved. International Copyright Secured. Used by Permission.

GIVE THANKS
Irregular

PRAISE AND THANKSGIVING

268 King of Kings

*The song may be repeated several times, getting faster each time.

WORDS and MUSIC: Naomi-Batya and Sophie Conty
© 1980 MARANATHA! MUSIC (Administered by THE COPYRIGHT COMPANY, Nashville, TN)
All Rights Reserved. International Copyright Secured. Used by Permission.

THE WORK OF THE SON

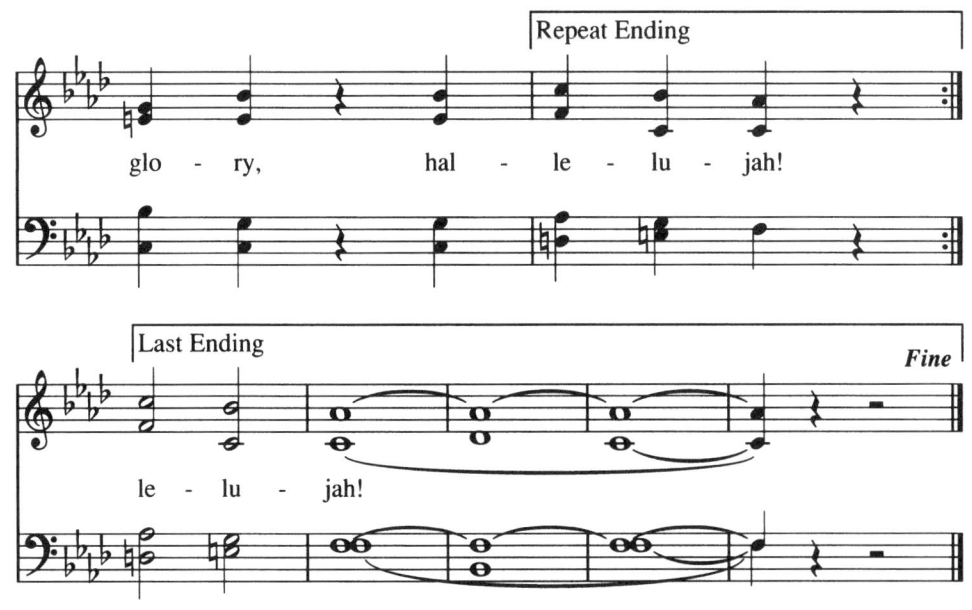

Let All That Is Within Me 269

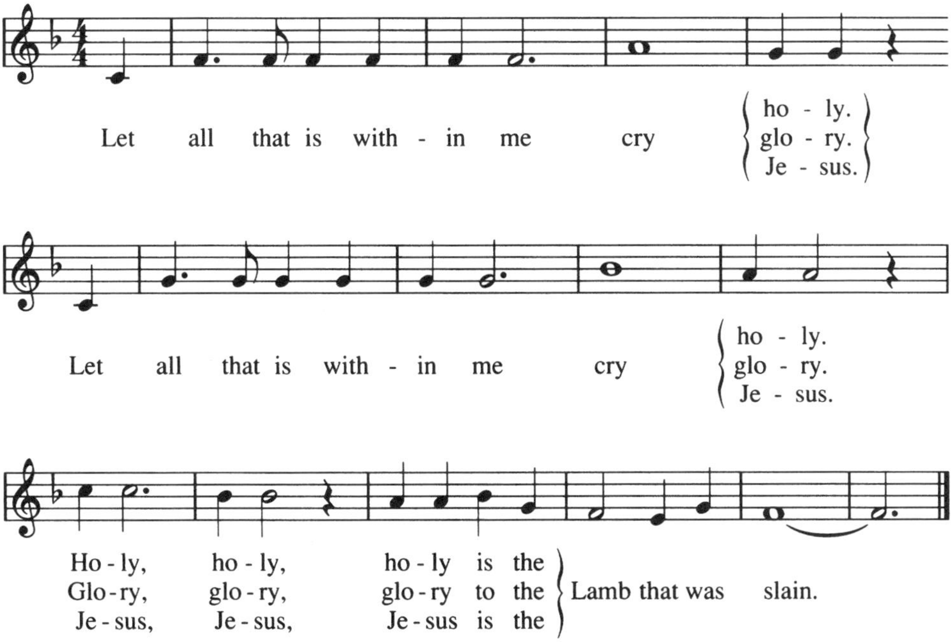

Let all that is with-in me cry { ho-ly. / glo-ry. / Je-sus. }

Let all that is with-in me cry { ho-ly. / glo-ry. / Je-sus. }

Ho-ly, ho-ly, ho-ly is the } Lamb that was slain.
Glo-ry, glo-ry, glo-ry to the
Je-sus, Je-sus, Je-sus is the

WORDS and MUSIC: Melvin Harrell
Copyright © 1963 by Gospel Publishing House. All Rights Reserved. Used by Permission

PRAISE AND THANKSGIVING

272 Amazing Love
♩ = 132

1. My Lord, what love is this that pays so dearly; that I, the guilty one may go free.
2. And so they watched Him die, despised, rejected; but O the blood He shed flowed for me.
3. And now this love of Christ shall flow like rivers; come wash your guilt away, live again.

A-mazing love, O what sacrifice, the Son of God,

WORDS and MUSIC: Graham Kendrick
© 1989 by Make Way Music/Adm. in N., S., & C. America by Integrity's Hosanna! Music.
c/o Integrity Music, Inc., P.O. Box 851622, Mobile, AL 36685
All Rights Reserved. International Copyright Secured. Used by Permission.

THE WORK OF THE SON

PRAISE AND THANKSGIVING

273 Jesus Is Our King

WORDS: Sherrell Prebble and Howard Clark
MUSIC: Sherrell Prebble
© 1978 CELEBRATION (Administered by THE COPYRIGHT COMPANY, Nashville, TN)
All Rights Reserved. International Copyright Secured. Used by Permission.

POST GREEN
Irregular, with Refrain

THE WORK OF THE SON

We See the Lord 274

WORDS: Based on Isaiah 6:1
MUSIC: Anonymous, Arr. Betty Pulkingham
Music arr. © 1971 CELEBRATION (Administered by THE COPYRIGHT COMPANY, Nashville, TN)
All Rights Reserved. International Copyright Secured. Used by Permission.

PRAISE AND THANKSGIVING

275 My Jesus, I Love Thee

1. My Jesus, I love thee, I know thou art mine, for thee all the follies of sin I resign; my gracious Redeemer, my Savior art thou; if ever I loved thee, my Jesus, 'tis now.
2. I love thee because thou hast first loved me, and purchased my pardon on Calvary's tree; I love thee for wearing the thorns on thy brow; if ever I loved thee, my Jesus, 'tis now.
3. In mansions of glory and endless delight, I'll ever adore thee in heaven so bright; I'll sing with the glittering crown on my brow: If ever I loved thee, my Jesus, 'tis now.

WORDS: William R. Featherstone, c. 1862
MUSIC: Adoniram J. Gordon, 1876

GORDON
11.11.11.11.

THE WORK OF THE SON

Soon and Very Soon 276

Unison or Three-Part

1., 3. Soon and ver-y soon, we are going to see the King;
2. No more dy-ing there, we are going to see the King;

soon and ver-y soon, we are going to see the King;
no more dy-ing there, we are going to see the King;

soon and ver-y soon, we are going to see the King; hal-le-
no more dy-ing there, we are going to see the King; hal-le-

lu-jah! Hal-le-lu-jah! We're going to see the King.

going to see the King! Hal-le-lu-jah! Hal-le-lu-jah!

WORDS and MUSIC: Andraé Crouch
© 1976 Bud John Songs, Inc./Crouch Music. Admin. by EMI Christian Music Publishing.
All Rights Reserved. International Copyright Secured. Used by Permission.

THE WORK OF THE SON

to bear the dread-ful curse for my soul?
Christ laid a-side his crown for my soul.
while mil-lions join the theme, I will sing.
and through e-ter-ni-ty I'll sing on.

Wait for the Lord 278

Refrain
Lento (♩ = 48)

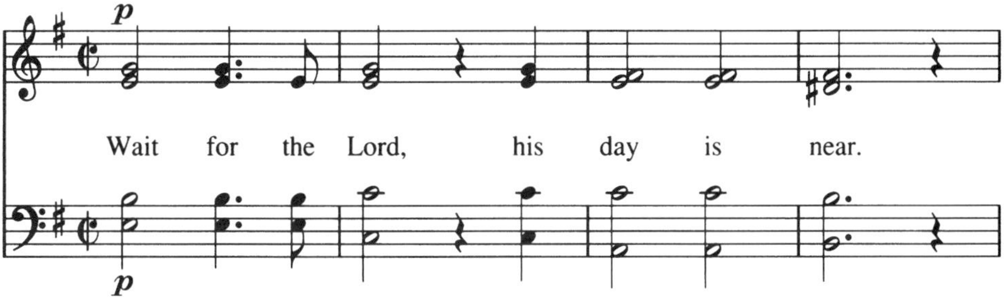

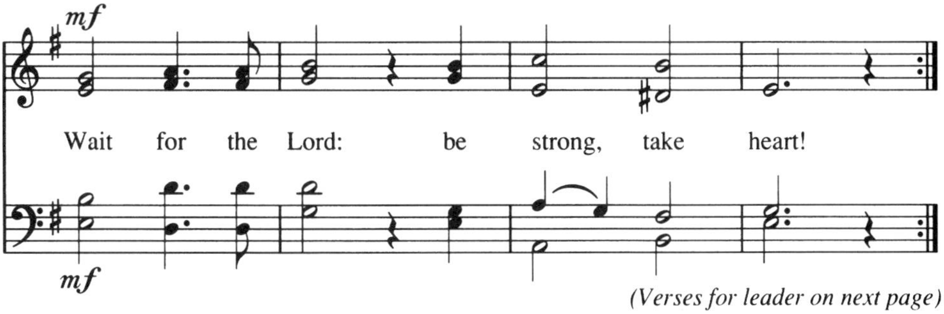

Wait for the Lord, his day is near.

Wait for the Lord: be strong, take heart!

(Verses for leader on next page)

WORDS: From Scripture
MUSIC: From the Taizé Community
Copyright © 1984 Les Presses de Taizé (France). Used by permission of G.I.A. Publications, Inc.,
Chicago, Illinois, exclusive agent. All Rights Reserved.

THE WORK OF THE SON

At the Name of Jesus 279

1. At the name of Je - sus ev - ery knee shall bow,
2. At his voice cre - a - tion sprang at once to sight:
3. Hum-bled for a sea - son, to re-ceive a name
4. bore it up tri - um - phant with its hu - man light,
5. In your hearts en - throne him; there let him sub - due
6. Chris-tians, this Lord Je - sus shall re - turn a - gain,

ev - ery tongue con - fess him King of glo - ry now;
all the an - gel fac - es, all the hosts of light,
from the lips of sin - ners, un - to whom he came;
through all ranks of crea - tures, to the cen - tral height,
all that is not ho - ly, all that is not true.
with his Fa - ther's glo - ry, o'er the earth to reign;

'tis the Fa - ther's plea - sure we should call him Lord,
thrones and dom - i - na - tions, stars up - on their way,
faith - ful - ly he bore it spot-less to the last,
to the throne of God - head, to the Fa - ther's breast;
Look to him, your Sav - ior, in temp - ta - tion's hour;
for all wreaths of em - pire meet up - on his brow,

who from the be - gin - ning was the might - y Word.
all the heav-enly or - ders in their great ar - ray.
brought it back vic - to - rious when from death he passed;
filled it with the glo - ry of that per - fect rest.
let his will en - fold you in its light and power.
and our hearts con - fess him King of glo - ry now.

WORDS: Caroline M. Noel
MUSIC: Ralph Vaughan Williams
Music used by permission of Oxford University Press from *Enlarged Songs of Praise 1931*.

KING'S WESTON
6.5.6.5.D.

Songs to Invoke the Presence of the Holy Spirit

✥ ✥ ✥

280 Like the Murmur of the Dove's Song

1. Like the mur-mur of the dove's song, like the chal-lenge of her flight, like the vig-or of the wind's rush, like the new flame's ea-ger might: Come, Ho-ly Spir-it, come.
2. To the mem-bers of Christ's bod-y, to the branch-es of the Vine, to the Church in faith as-sem-bled, to her midst as gift and sign: Come, Ho-ly Spir-it, come.
3. With the heal-ing of di-vi-sion, with the cease-less voice of prayer, with the power to love and wit-ness, with the peace be-yond com-pare: Come, Ho-ly Spir-it, come.

WORDS: Carl P. Daw, Jr., 1982
MUSIC: Peter Cutts, 1969
Words © 1982 by Hope Publishing Co.
Music © 1969 Hope Publishing Co., Carol Stream, IL 60188. All Rights Reserved.

BRIDEGROOM

THE PRESENCE OF THE HOLY SPIRIT

Come, Holy Spirit 281

WORDS and MUSIC: Mark Foreman
© 1982 Mercy Publishing.

PRAISE AND THANKSGIVING

282 There's a Spirit in the Air

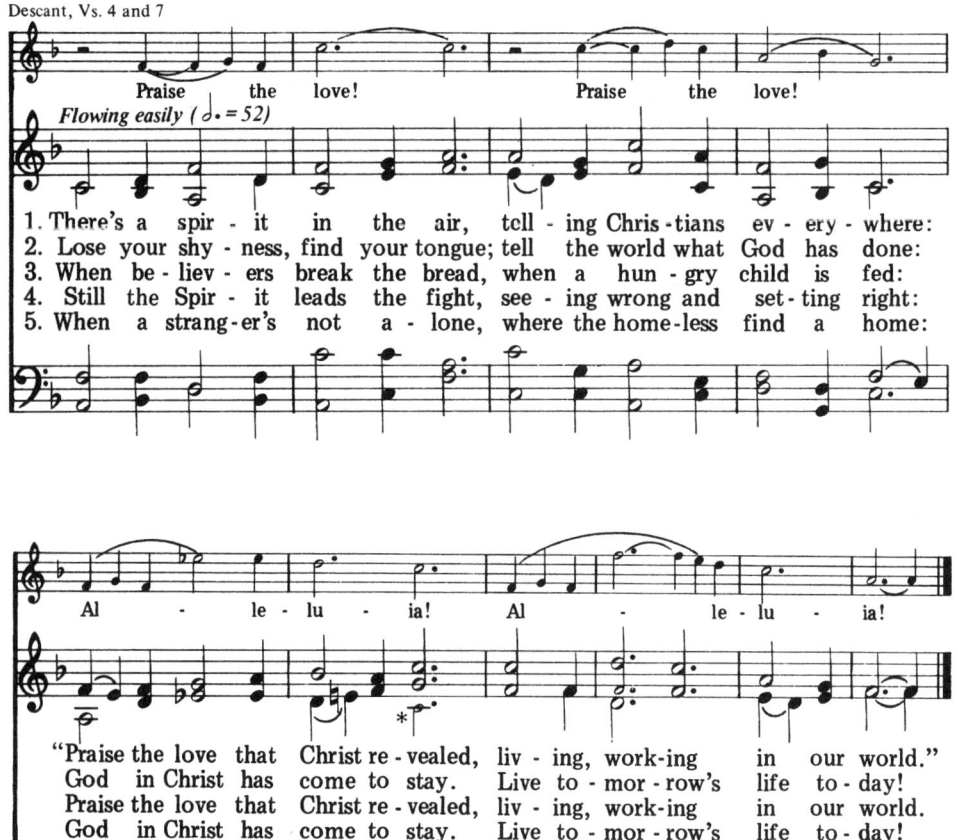

6. May the Spirit fill our praise,
   guide our thoughts and change our ways.
   God in Christ has come to stay.
   Live tomorrow's life today!

7. There's a Spirit in the air,
   calling people everywhere:
   Praise the love that Christ revealed,
   living, working in our world.

WORDS: Brian Wren, 1969
MUSIC: John W. Wilson, 1969
Copyright © 1979 by Hope Publishing Co., Carol Stream, IL 60188. All Rights Reserved.

LAUDS
7.7.7.7.

THE PRESENCE OF THE HOLY SPIRIT

Creating Spirit, Holy Lord 283

1. Creating Spirit, holy Lord, the gentle breeze, the mighty wind, with warmth and pow'r and graciousness in grace refashion heart and mind.
2. O Comforter of all who toil, gift from the fountainhead of light, O Spirit of all love and fire, anointing chrism of all might.
3. O molder of our freedom strong and gentle finger of God's hand, come, lead our words within the paths that wisdom in your love has planned.
4. Alert our senses, touch our hearts and fire us with your gift of love, that proud and fallen, weak and blind, your light may lead us from above.
5. Drive far into their darkness all who shun your living gifts of peace; protect us deep within your calm and keep us safe till dangers cease.

6. Through you may we in silence find
a deeper knowledge of God's Son;
through you we know the Father's love
and live by faith till night is gone.

7. All glory to the Father's Son
who from the grave has ris'n on high;
his Spirit makes us sing with joy
and praise our God eternally.

WORDS: *Veni, Creator Spiritus*; Tr. by Ralph Wright
MUSIC: Trier manuscript, 15th C.; adapt. Michael Praetorius, 1609; harm. George R. Woodward, 1910
Words trans. copyright © 1989 by G.I.A. Publications, Inc., Chicago, Illinois.
All Rights Reserved. Used by Permission.

PUER NOBIS
LM

PRAISE AND THANKSGIVING

284 Now Holy Spirit, Ever One

Now Holy Spirit, ever one

with God the Father and the Son,

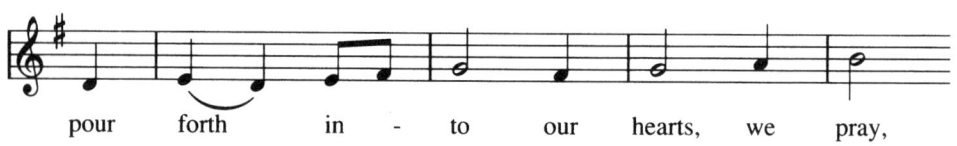
pour forth into our hearts, we pray,

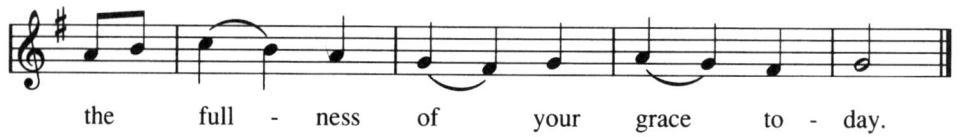
the fullness of your grace today.

WORDS: Ambrose of Milan; versified in *The Hymnal 1982*
MUSIC: William Knapp, 1738
Harmonization by Emily R. Brink, 1994. © 1994, CRC Publications, Grand Rapids, MI 49560.
All Rights Reserved. Used by Permission.

WAREHAM
LM

The Going Forth

Songs of Service

285 May the Mind of Christ, My Savior

WORDS: Kate B. Wilkinson, 1925
MUSIC: A. Cyril Barham-Gould, 1925; desc. Emily R. Brink, 1986.
Descant by Emily R. Brink, © 1987, CRC Publications, Grand Rapids, MI 49560.
All Rights Reserved. Used by Permission.

ST. LEONARDS
87 85

SONGS OF SERVICE

We Are the Light of the World 288

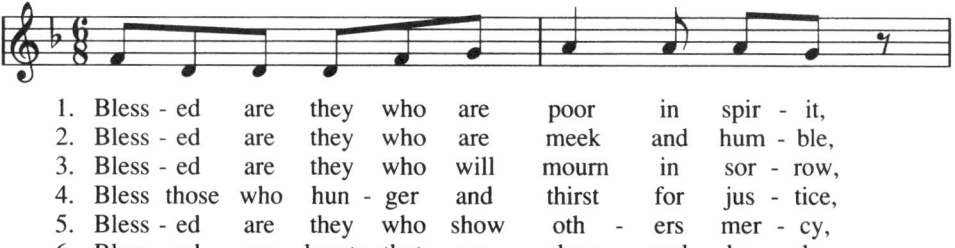

1. Bless - ed are they who are poor in spir - it,
2. Bless - ed are they who are meek and hum - ble,
3. Bless - ed are they who will mourn in sor - row,
4. Bless those who hun - ger and thirst for jus - tice,
5. Bless - ed are they who show oth - ers mer - cy,
6. Bless - ed are hearts that are clean and ho - ly,
7. Bless - ed are they who bring peace a - mong us,
8. Bless those who suf - fer from per - se - cu - tion,

1. Theirs is the King-dom of God. Bless us, O Lord, make us
2. They will in - her - it the earth. Bless us, O Lord, make us
3. They will be com - fort - ed. Bless us, O Lord, when we
4. They will be sat - is - fied. Bless us, O Lord, hear our
5. They will know mer - cy too. Bless us, O Lord, hear our
6. They will be - hold the Lord. Bless us, O Lord, make us
7. They are the chil - dren of God. Bless us, O Lord, may your
8. Theirs is the King-dom of God. Bless us, O Lord, when they

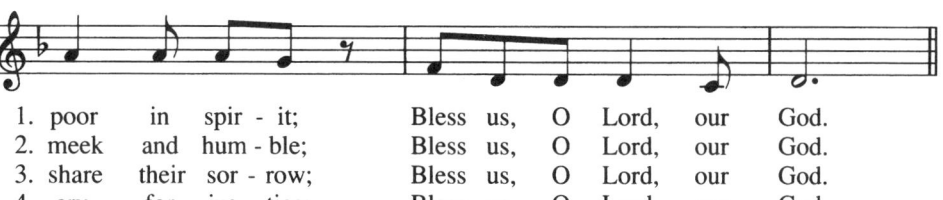

1. poor in spir - it; Bless us, O Lord, our God.
2. meek and hum - ble; Bless us, O Lord, our God.
3. share their sor - row; Bless us, O Lord, our God.
4. cry for jus - tice; Bless us O Lord, our God.
5. cry for mer - cy; Bless us, O Lord, our God.
6. pure and ho - ly; Bless us, O Lord, our God.
7. peace be with us; Bless us, O Lord, our God.
8. per - se - cute us; Bless us, O Lord, our God.

We are the light of the world, may our light shine be-fore all,

That they may see the good that we do, and give glo - ry to God.

WORDS and MUSIC: Jean Anthony Greif
Words and Music © 1966, Vernacular Hymns Publishing Co.

SONGS OF SERVICE

Go Forth in His Name 290

1. We are His chil-dren, the fruit of His suf-f'ring,
2. Count-less the souls that are stum-bling in dark-ness,
3. Lis-ten, the wind of the Spir-it is blow-ing, the

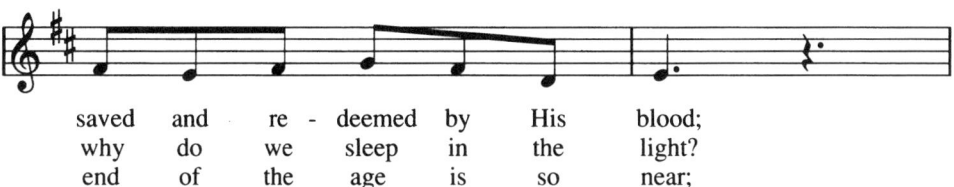

saved and re - deemed by His blood;
why do we sleep in the light?
end of the age is so near;

Called to be ho - ly, a light to the na - tions,
Je - sus com-mands us to go make dis - ci - ples,
Pow'rs in the earth and the heav - ens are shak - ing,

(Turn for Chorus)

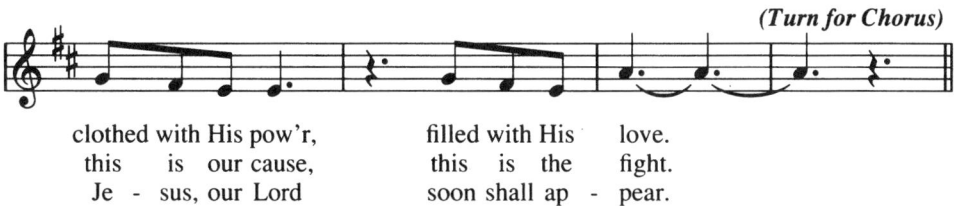

clothed with His pow'r, filled with His love.
this is our cause, this is the fight.
Je - sus, our Lord soon shall ap - pear.

WORDS and MUSIC: Graham Kendrick
© 1990 Make Way Music/Adm. in N., S., & C. America by Integrity's Hosanna! Music.
c/o Integrity Music, Inc., P.O. Box 851622, Mobile, AL 36685.
All Rights Reserved. International Copyright Secured. Used by Permission.

THE GOING FORTH

Go forth in His name, proclaiming

"Jesus reigns." Now is the time for the church to arise and pro-

claim Him, "Jesus, Savior, Redeemer and Lord."

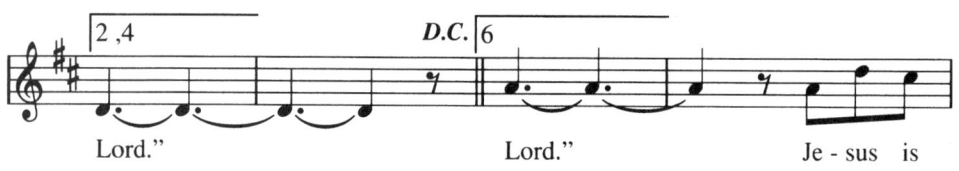
Lord."   Lord."   Jesus is

Lord,   Jesus is Lord.

291 Go Forth for God

1. Go forth for God, go to the world in peace;
2. Go forth for God, go to the world in love;
3. Go forth for God, go to the world in strength;
4. Go forth for God, go to the world in joy,

WORDS: J. R. Peacey
MUSIC: *Genevan Psalter*, 1551; harm. by C. Winfred Douglas, alt.
Words © 1984 by Hope Publishing Co., Carol Stream, IL 60188. All Rights Reserved.

GENEVA 124
10 10.10 10.10

Benedictions

292 Bind Us Together

Bind us to-geth-er, Lord, bind us to-geth-er with cords that can-not be bro-ken.
Bind us to-geth-er, Lord, bind us to-geth-er, bind us to-geth-er in love.

Fine

There is on-ly one God, there is on-ly one King; there is on-ly one bo-dy, that is why we sing:

D.C. al Fine

WORDS and MUSIC: Bob Gillman
© 1984 Kingsway's Thankyou Music/Adm. in N., S., & C. America by Integrity's Hosanna! Music.

BENEDICTIONS

Go Now in Peace 293
(Canon)

WORDS and MUSIC: Natalie Sleeth
Copyright © 1976 Hinshaw Music, Inc. Reprinted by Permission.

GO IN PEACE
IRREGULAR

Shalom, My Friends, Shalom 294

WORDS: Israeli round; English version, Donald P. Hustad, 1988
MUSIC: Hebrew melody
English words © 1990 by Hope Publishing Co., Carol Stream, IL 60188. All Rights Reserved.

SHALOM CHAVERIM
Irregular

THE GOING FORTH

295 Lord, Bid Your Servant Go in Peace

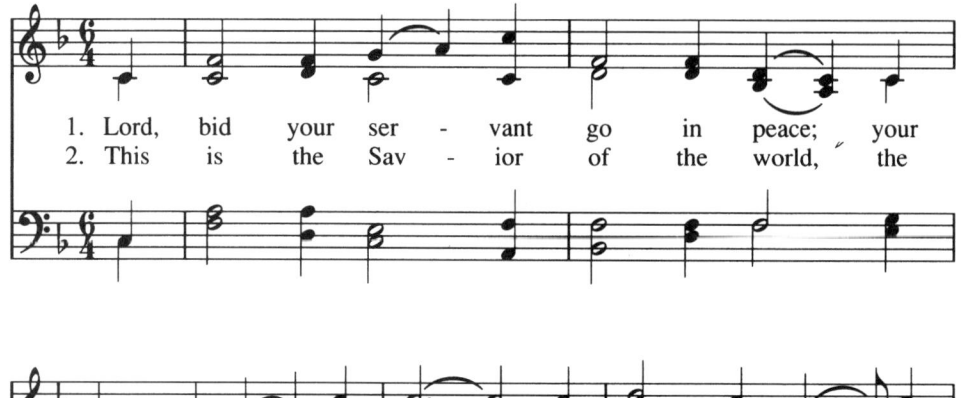

1. Lord, bid your ser - vant go in peace; your
2. This is the Sav - ior of the world, the

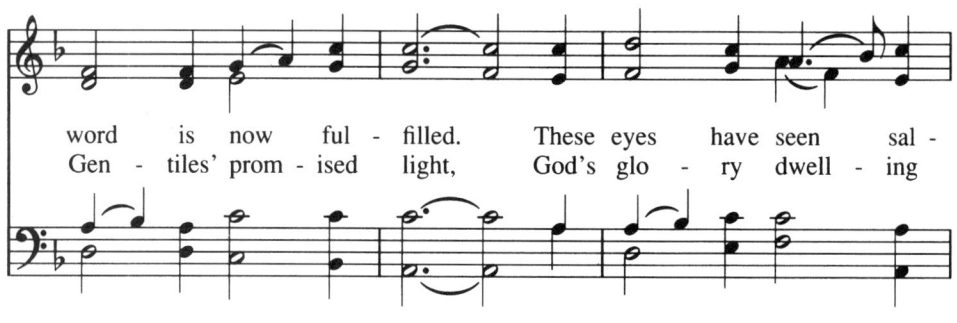

word is now ful - filled. These eyes have seen sal -
Gen - tiles' prom - ised light, God's glo - ry dwell - ing

va - tion's dawn, this child so long fore - told.
in our midst, the joy of Is - ra - el.

WORDS: *Song of Simeon* (Luke 2:29-32); Para. James Quinn, S.J., 1969
MUSIC: American Folk Tune; Harm. Russell Schulz-Widmar, 1983 (from *Songs for the People of God*).
Para. © 1969, James Quinn. Used by permission of Selah Publishing Co., Inc., North American agent.
Harm. © 1994, Selah Publishing Co., Inc., Kingston, NY 12401.
All Rights Reserved. Used by Permission.

LAND OF REST
CM

Recessional Hymns

Jesus Shall Reign 296

1. Jesus shall reign where'er the sun does its successive journeys run; his kingdom spread from shore to shore, till moons shall wax and wane no more.
2. To him shall endless prayer be made, and endless praises crown his head; his name like sweet perfume shall rise with every morning sacrifice.
3. People and realms of every tongue dwell on his love with sweetest song, and infant voices shall proclaim their early blessings on his name.
4. Blessings abound where'er he reigns; the prisoners leap to lose their chains, the weary find eternal rest, and all who suffer want are blessed.
5. Let all the people rise and bring their special honors to our King; angels descend with songs again and earth repeat the loud Amen.

WORDS: Isaac Watts, 1719, alt.; para. of Psalm 72
MUSIC: John Hatton, 1793

DUKE STREET
L.M.

THE GOING FORTH

297 Lift High the Cross

WORDS: George W. Kitchin, 1887; rev. Michael R. Newbolt, 1916, alt.
MUSIC: Sydney H. Nicholson, 1916
Copyright © 1974 by Hope Publishing Co., Carol Stream, IL 60188. All Rights Reserved.

CRUCIFER
10.10.10.10.

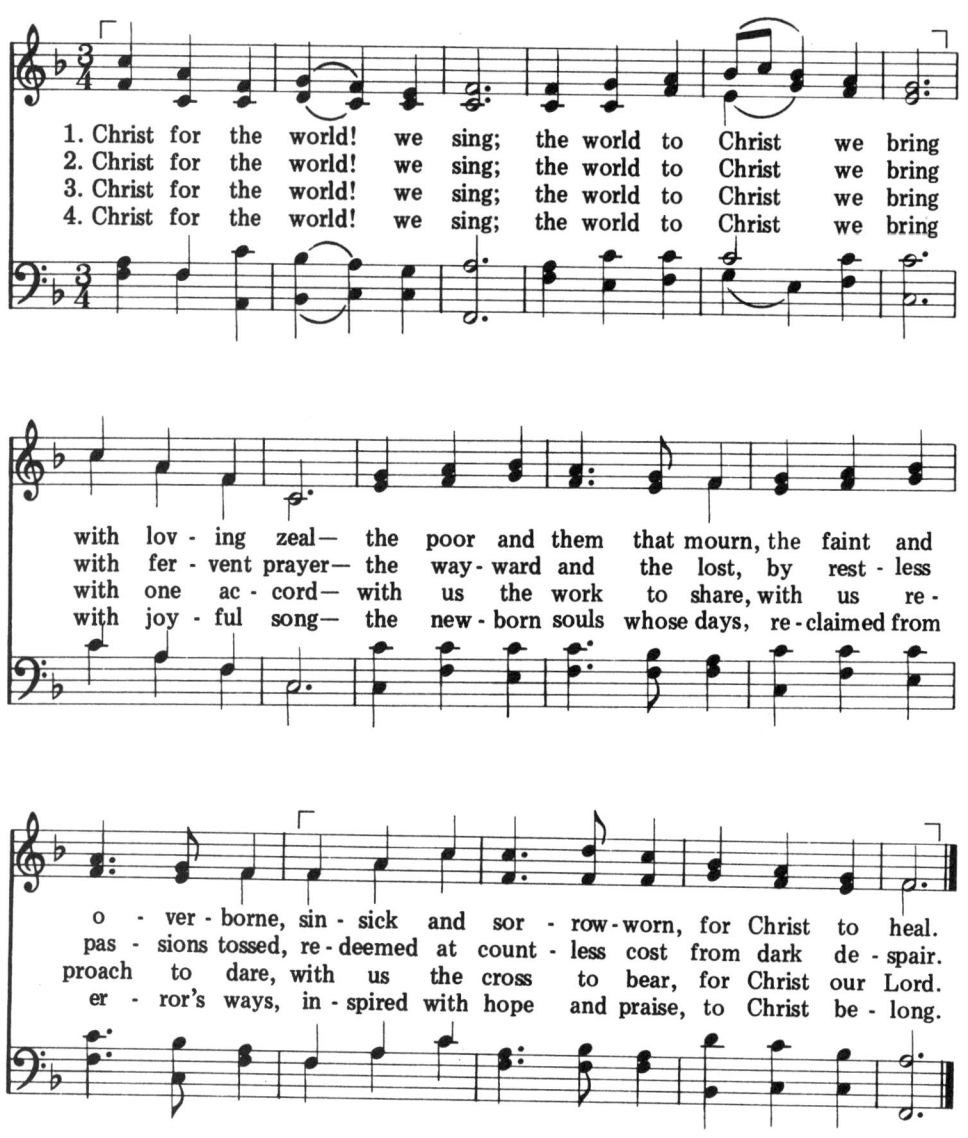

RECESSIONAL HYMNS

Christ Is Alive! 300

1. Christ is alive! Let Christians sing. The cross stands empty to the sky. Let streets and homes with praises ring. Love, drowned in death, shall never die.
2. Christ is alive! No longer bound to distant years in Palestine, but saving, healing, here and now, and touching every place and time.
3. In every insult, rift and war, where color, scorn or wealth divide, Christ suffers still, yet loves the more, and lives, where even hope has died.
4. Women and men, in age and youth, can feel the Spirit, hear the call, and find the way, the life, the truth, revealed in Jesus, freed for all.
5. Christ is alive, and comes to bring good news to this and every age, till earth and sky and ocean ring with joy, with justice, love and praise.

WORDS: Brian Wren, 1968
MUSIC: Thomas Williams' *Psalmodia Evangelica*, 1789
Words © 1975 by Hope Publishing Co., Carol Stream, IL 60188. All Rights Reserved.

TRURO
L.M.

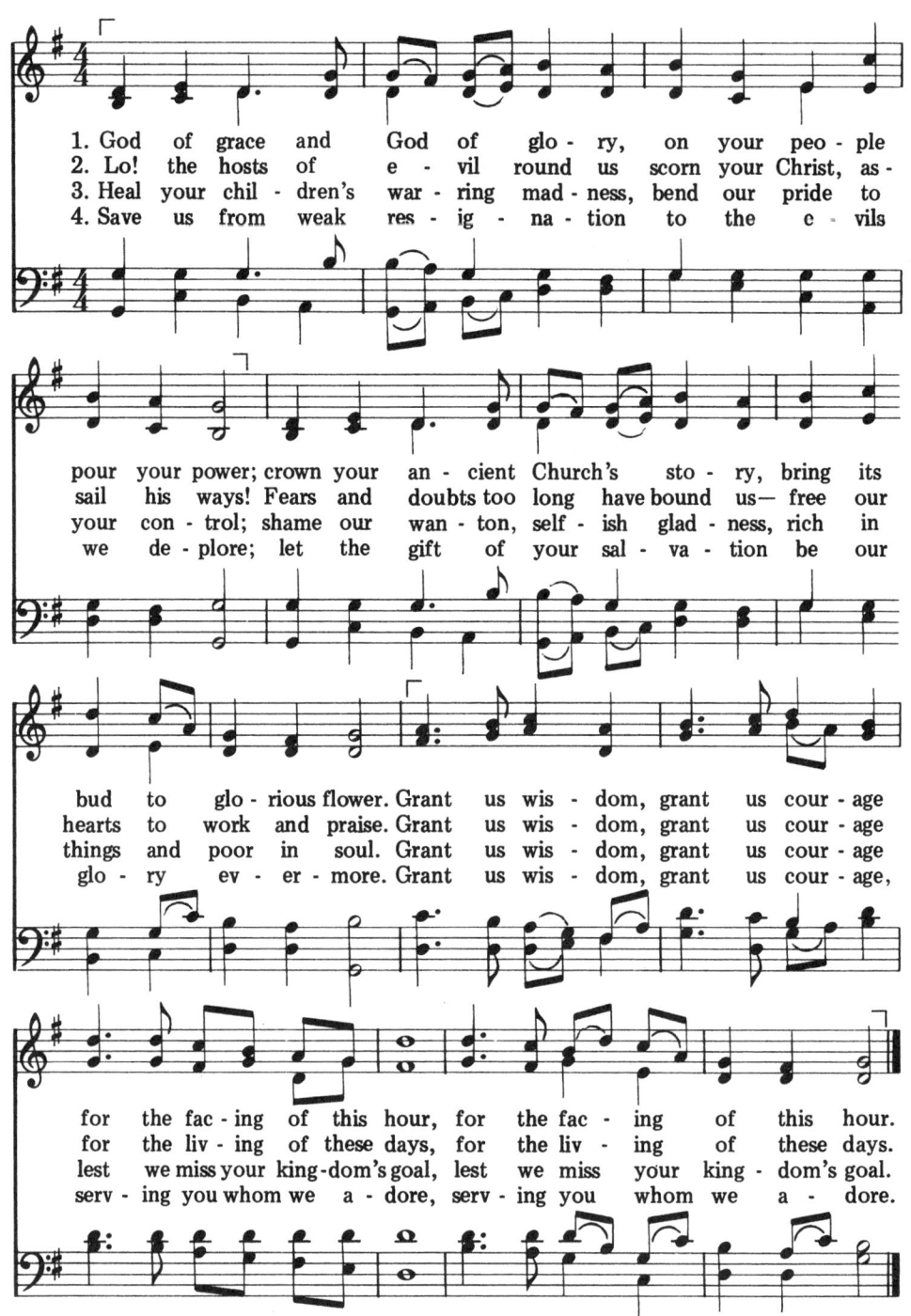

RECESSIONAL HYMNS

The Trees of the Field 302

* ✗ = clap hands.

WORDS: Isaiah 55:12, adapt. by Steffi Geiser Rubin, 1975
MUSIC: Stuart Dauermann, 1975
© 1975 LILLENAS PUBLISHING COMPANY (Administered by THE COPYRIGHT COMPANY, Nashville, TN) All Rights Reserved. International Copyright Secured. Used by Permission.

THE TREES OF THE FIELD
Irregular

THE GOING FORTH

303 Song for the Nations

Moderately slow, majestic (♩ = 63)

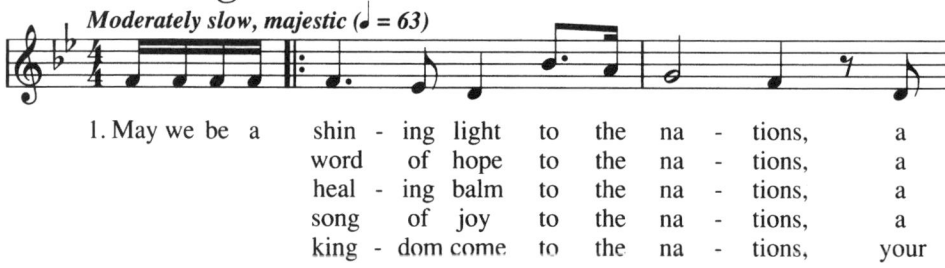

1. May we be a shin - ing light to the na - tions, a
   word of hope to the na - tions, a
   heal - ing balm to the na - tions, a
   song of joy to the na - tions, a
   king - dom come to the na - tions, your

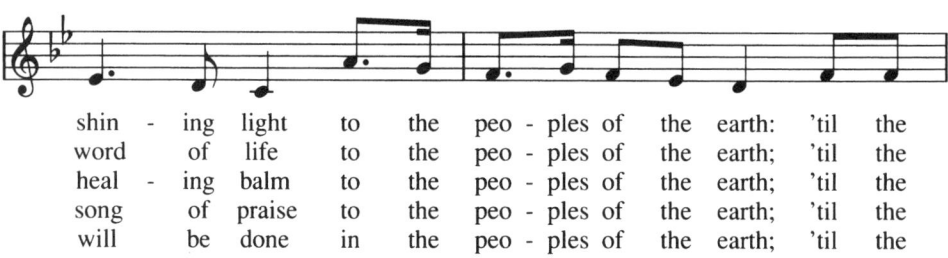

shin - ing light to the peo - ples of the earth; 'til the
word of life to the peo - ples of the earth; 'til the
heal - ing balm to the peo - ples of the earth; 'til the
song of praise to the peo - ples of the earth; 'til the
will be done in the peo - ples of the earth; 'til the

whole world sees the glo - ry of your name.
whole world knows there's sal - va - tion through your name.
whole world knows the pow - er of your name.
whole world rings with the prais - es of your name.
whole world knows that Je - sus Christ is Lord.

(Fine)

May your pure light shine through us! 2. May we bring a
May your mer - cy flow through us! 3. May we be a
May your heal - ing flow through us! 4. May we sing a
May your song be sung through us! 5. May your
May your king - dom come on earth!

WORDS and MUSIC: Chris Christensen
© 1986 Integrity's Hosanna! Music. c/o Integrity Music, Inc., P.O. Box 851622, Mobile, AL 36685.
All Rights Reserved. International Copyright Secured. Used by Permission

RECESSIONAL HYMNS

Send Us Out 304

Send us out to proclaim the reign of your kingdom,

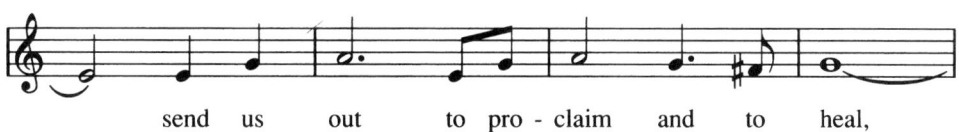
send us out to proclaim and to heal,

send us out with your power and your authority

to overcome and to heal the world.

WORDS and MUSIC: John Michael Talbot
© 1984 Birdwing Music/Cherry Lane Music Publishing Co., Inc.
Admin. by EMI Christian Music Publishing.
International Copyright Secured. All Rights Reserved

THE GOING FORTH

305 Lord, You Give the Great Commission

1. Lord, you give the great com-mis-sion: "Heal the sick and
2. Lord, you call us to your ser-vice: "In my name bap-
3. Lord, you make the com-mon ho-ly: "This my bod-y,
4. Lord, you show us love's true meas-ure: "Fa-ther, what they
5. Lord, you bless with words as-sur-ing: "I am with you

preach the word." Lest the church ne-glect its mis-sion
tize and teach." That the world may trust your prom-ise,
this my blood." Let us all, for earth's true glo-ry,
do, for-give." Yet we hoard as pri-vate treas-ure
to the end." Faith and hope and love re-stor-ing,

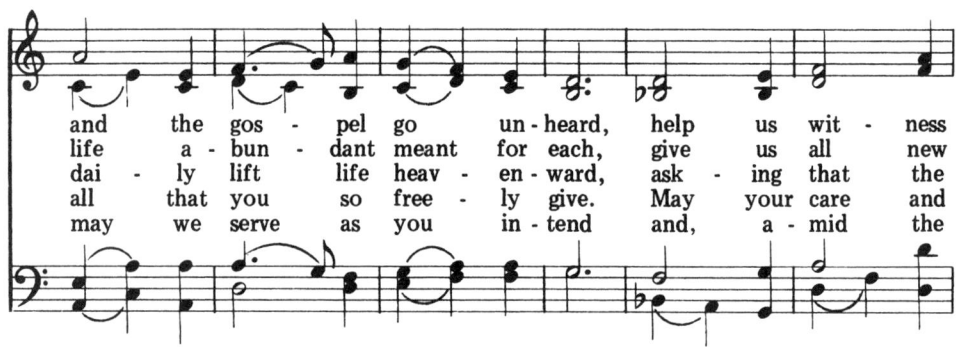

and the gos-pel go un-heard, help us wit-ness
life a-bun-dant meant for each, give us all new
dai-ly lift life heav-en-ward, ask-ing that the
all that you so free-ly give. May your care and
may we serve as you in-tend and, a-mid the

WORDS: Jeffery Rowthorn, 1978
MUSIC: Cyril V. Taylor, 1941
Words © 1978 by Hope Publishing Co. Music © 1942,
renewal 1970 by Hope Publishing Co., Carol Stream, IL 60188. All Rights Reserved.

ABBOT'S LEIGH
8.7.8.7.D.

RECESSIONAL HYMNS

to your pur-pose with re-newed in-teg-ri-ty:
fer-vor, draw us clos-er in com-mu-ni-ty:
world a-round us share your chil-dren's lib-er-ty:
mer-cy lead us to a just so-ci-e-ty:
cares that claim us, hold in mind e-ter-ni-ty:

Refrain

With the Spir-it's gifts em-power us for the work of min-is-try.

THE GOING FORTH

306 We Are Marching in the Light of the Lord

WORDS and MUSIC: Zulu Traditional Song
Arranged by Hal H. Hopson
Copyright © 1984 by Utryck. Used by permission of Walton Music Corporation.

RECESSIONAL HYMNS

THE GOING FORTH

308 Send Me, Jesus
Thuma mina

1. Thuma mina
   Thuma mina, thuma mina
   Thuma mina, somandla

2. Roma nna
   roma nna, roma nna
   roma nna, modimo

WORDS and MUSIC: South African
Copyright © 1984 Utryck. Used by permission of Walton Music Corporation.

THUMA MINA
Irregular

Alphabetical Index of Hymns

A Round for Peace	240
(Dona Nobis Pacem)	
A Shield About Me	100
Abba Father	264
Ah, Holy Jesus	183
Ah, Lord God	254
All Creatures of Our God and King	47
All Hail King Jesus	35
All Hail the Power of Jesus' Name	45
All Heaven Declares	163
Alleluia	136
Alleluia	138
Alleluia, Alleluia, Give Thanks	271
Alleluia, Sing to Jesus	58
Amazing Grace! How Sweet the Sound	189
Amazing Love	272
(My Lord What Love Is This)	
And Can It Be That I Should Gain	193
Arise, Shine, for Your Light Is Come	123
As Moses Raised the Serpent Up	132
As the Deer Pants for the Water	9
As We Gather	6
At the Name of Jesus	279
(KING'S WESTON)	
At the Name of Jesus	133
(CAMBERWELL)	
Awake, O Israel	259
Awesome God	245
Be Not Afraid	243
Be Still and Know That I Am God	10
Be Still for the Spirit of the Lord	201
Be Thou My Vision	151
Bind Us Together	292
Bless His Holy Name	16
Bless the Lord	114
Blessed Be the God of Israel	128
Blessed Be the Name of the Lord	260
Blessed Jesus, at Your Word	93
Blessing, Honor and Glory	81
Blest Are They	127
Bring Forth the Kingdom	153
(You Are Salt for the Earth)	
Broken for Me	218
By the Waters	88
Canta, Débora, Canta!	121
Cantad al Señor	74
Oh Sing to the Lord	
Cantemos al Señor	11
Let's Sing unto the Lord	
Change My Heart, O God	143
Christ Beside Me	164
Christ for the World! We Sing	299
Christ Has Died	210
Christ Has Died, Christ Is Risen	209
Christ Has Died (HAUGEN)	212
Christ Is Alive!	300
Come and Rejoice	20
(Come with Rejoicing)	
Come, Christians, Join to Sing	50
Come, Holy Spirit	281
Come into His Presence	2
Come, Let Us Eat	197
Come, Let Us Reason	190
Come, Let Us with Our Lord Arise	18
Come Quickly, Lord	110
Come, Ye Sinners, Poor and Needy	141
Create in Me a Clean Heart	181
Create in Me a Clean Heart	182
Creating Spirit, Holy Lord	283
Crown Him with Many Crowns	56
Dona Nobis Pacem	240
Dona Nobis Pacem Domine	241
Doxology	82
Eat This Bread	228
Emmanuel	28
Every Eye Shall See	162
Fairest Lord Jesus	166
Fear Not, Rejoice and Be Glad	124
Forgive Our Sins as We Forgive	184
Freely, Freely	192
Gift of Finest Wheat	217
(You Satisfy the Hungry Heart)	
Give Thanks with a Grateful Heart	266
Give to Our God Immortal Praise	255
Gloria, Gloria	64
Glorify Your Name	37
(Father, We Love You)	
Glory Be to Jesus	233
Glory Be to the Father	67
Glory to God	66

ALPHABETICAL INDEX

Glory to God, Glory in the Highest	65
Glory to the Lamb	135
Go Forth for God	291
Go Forth in His Name	290
(We Are His Children)	
Go Now in Peace	293
God Himself Is with Us	8
God Is Here!	5
God Is My Great Desire	109
God of Grace and God of Glory	301
God's Holy Ways Are Just and True	115
Great Are You, Lord	69
(Holy Lord, Most Holy Lord)	
Great Is the Lord	22
Great Is Thy Faithfulness	249
Hail to the Lord's Anointed	101
Halle, Halle, Hallelujah	139
Hallelujah, My Father	200
Hallelujah, Praise the Lord	119
Hallelujah, We Sing Your Praises	239
He Is Exalted	238
He Is Lord	29
He Who Began a Good Work	134
Healer of My Soul	224
Hear My Cry	108
Hear, O Lord, My Urgent Prayer	104
Heleluyan	137
(Alleluia)	
Here I Am, Lord	149
Here in this Place	14
His Name Is Wonderful	30
Holy, Holy	206
Holy, Holy, Holy	208
Santo, Santo, Santo	
Holy, Holy, Holy Is the Lord of Hosts	205
Holy, Holy, Holy Lord	207
Holy, Holy, Holy! Lord God Almighty	204
Holy Is the Lord	203
Holy Spirit, Mighty God	95
Hosanna	71
Hosanna to the Living King!	72
(I Will Praise the Lord with Harp and String)	
Hosea	126
(Come Back to Me)	
How Blessed Are You	231
How Great Thou Art	250
How Long, O Lord	87
How Majestic Is Your Name	98
Humble Thyself in the Sight of the Lord	188
I Am the Bread of Life	246
I Bind Unto Myself Today	165
I Cannot Tell	160
I Come with Joy	195
I Exalt Thee	44
I Love You, Lord	36
I Love You Lord, My Strength, My Rock	105
I Rejoiced When I Heard Them Say	117
I Sing Praises	79
I Sing the Mighty Power of God	54
I Want to Walk as a Child of the Light	152
I Will Call Upon the Lord	15
I Will Celebrate	77
I Will Change Your Name	225
I Will Exalt My God, My King	78
Te Exaltaré Mi Dios, Mi Rey	
I Will Sing of the Mercies	111
I Will Sing unto the Lord	120
If My People	186
If You Belive and I Believe	168
Immortal, Invisible, God Only Wise	46
In the Presence of Your People	12
Je Louerai l'Eternel	76
Praise, I Will Praise You, Lord	
Jehovah-Jireh	24
Jesu, Jesu, Fill Us with Your Love	289
Jesus Is Our King	273
(Alleluia Alleluia Opening Our Hearts to Him)	
Jesus, Lamb of God	215
Jesus, Name Above All Names	26
Jesus, Remember Me	227
Jesus Shall Reign	296
Jesus, Stand Among Us	17
Jesus, Stand Among Us	237
Join All the Glorious Names	270
Jonah's Song	125
(In My Trouble)	
Just As I Am, without One Plea	140
King of Kings	268
King of the Nations	19
(Come Let Us Worship Jesus)	
Kyrie eleison	86
Lamb of God	214
Lead Me, Guide Me	176
Lead Me, Lord	175
Lead On, O King Eternal	298
Let All Mortal Flesh Keep Silence	229
Let All That Is Within Me	269
Let All Things Now Living	48
Let the Hungry Come to Me	220
Let the Whole Creation Cry	49
Let Us Pray to the Lord	171
Lift High the Cross	297
Lift Up Your Heads	73

ALPHABETICAL INDEX

Lift Up Your Heads, O Mighty Gates	59
Lift Your Heart to the Lord	61
Like the Murmur of the Dove's Song	280
Lord, Be Glorified	172
Lord, Bid Your Servant Go in Peace	295
Lord God, Almighty	40
Lord Have Mercy	84
Lord, Have Mercy upon Us	85
Lord, I Lift Your Name on High	4
Lord, I Want to Be a Christian	145
Lord of All Hopefulness	174
Lord, Whose Love in Humble Service	286
Lord, You Give the Great Commission	305
Love Divine, All Loves Excelling	196
Magnify the Lord	131
Majesty	63
Make Way	60
May the Mind of Christ, My Savior	285
Meekness and Majesty	158
My Jesus, I Love Thee	275
My Tribute	68
Now Holy Spirit, Ever One	284
Now Let Us from This Table Rise	242
Now the Silence, Then the Glory	221
O Christ, the Healer, We Have Come	191
O Christ, the Lamb of God	216
O Christe Domine Jesu	230
(O Christ, Lord Jesus)	
O Come, Let Us Adore Him	1
O for a Thousand Tongues to Sing	32
O How He Loves You and Me	27
O Lord Hear My Prayer	173
O Lord, My God, You Know All My Ways	118
O Lord, Your Tenderness	146
O Sacred Head, Now Wounded	235
O the Blood of Jesus	219
O Word of God Incarnate	97
Obey My Voice	142
Of the Father's Love Begotten	252
On Eagle's Wings	112
Open Our Eyes, Lord	91
Our Father	179
(Pater noster)	
Our Father Who Art in Heaven	178
Our Great Savior	194
Planted by the Waters	103
(Blessed Is the One Who Trusts in the Lord)	
Praise God From Whom All Blessings Flow	83
Praise, I Will Praise You, Lord	76
Praise, My Soul, the King of Heaven	53
Praise the Lord! O Heavens, Adore Him	75
Praise the Lord Who Reigns Above	253
Praise the Name of Jesus	7
Praise to the Lord, the Almighty	57
Praise to You, O God of Mercy	257
Prepare the Way	92
Purify My Heart	187
Righteous One	31
(Shining Like the Morning Sun)	
Rock of My Salvation	263
Sanctuary	185
(Lord Prepare Me to be a Sanctuary)	
Seekers of Your Heart	222
Send Me, Jesus (*Thuma Mina*)	308
Send Us Out	304
Sent by the Lord	154
Sent Forth by God's Blessing	307
Shalom, My Friends, Shalom	294
Shine, Jesus, Shine	247
Sing a New Song	21
Sing a New Song to the Lord	113
Sing Alleluia to the Lord	202
Sing, My Soul	129
(Mary's Song of Praise)	
Sing of the Lord's Goodness	256
Sing Praise to God Who Reigns Above	52
Sing Praise to the Father	251
Sing to the Lord a New Song	99
Soften My Heart	223
Softly and Tenderly Jesus Is Calling	147
Song for the Nations	303
(May We Be a Shining Light)	
Soon and Very Soon	276
Speak, Lord, in the Stillness	96
Spirit of the Living God	90
Spirit Song	248
Stay Here	170
Stay with Me	169
Surely It Is God Who Saves Me	122
(The First Song of Isaiah)	
Surely the Presence of the Lord	167
Take My Life That It May Be	150
Tell Out, My Soul	130
The Battle Belongs to the Lord	244
The City Is Alive, O God	89
The Gathering	13
The Gift of Love	155
The God of Abraham Praise	51
The Highest Place	39
The King of Glory	267
The King of Love	106
The Lord Is My Light	102
The Lord Is Present	55

The Lord's Prayer	177	We Are Marching in the Light	306
The Lord's Prayer (*West Indian*)	180	of the Lord	
The Servant Song	148	**We Are the Light of the World**	288
(Brother, Let Me Be Your Servant)		We Believe (in God the Father)	156
The Steadfast Love of the Lord	23	We Believe in God Almighty	157
The Threefold Truth	213	**We Bow Down**	38
The Trees of the Field	302	(You Are Lord of Creation)	
There Is a Redeemer	232	We Bring the Sacrifice of Praise	3
There Is One Lord	161	We Choose the Fear of the Lord	144
There's a Spirit in the Air	282	We Remember His Death	211
There's No God as Great	261	We See the Lord	274
No Hay Dios tan Grande		We Will Glorify	33
This Is the Feast	198	What a Mighty God	159
This Is the Feast of Victory	199	What Shall I Render to the Lord?	116
Thou Art Worthy	34	What Wondrous Love	277
Through Our God, We Shall	262	When I Look into Your Holiness	41
Do Valiantly		When I Survey the Wondrous Cross	236
Thy Word	94	When in Our Music God Is Glorified	62
To God Be the Glory	258	Worthy Is Christ	80
To Him Who Sits on the Throne	265	Digno Es Jesús	
Ubi Caritas et Amor	226	Worthy Is the Lamb	234
(Where Charity and Love Are		Worthy, You Are Worthy	43
Found, God Is There)		You Are My God	42
Victory Song	262	You Are My Hiding Place	107
(Through Our God, We Shall		You Have Been Given	70
Do Valiantly)		**You Have Been Good**	25
Wait for the Lord	278	Your Love Is Changing the World	287